The Children's
Music Book

Performing Musicians in School

by Saville Kushner

Calouste Gulbenkian
Foundation, London 1991

Dedication

To: Ike, Minnie, Iris and Alfonso...and Ame, of course

Biographical note

Saville Kushner is an educational researcher working at the Centre for Applied Research in Education (University of East Anglia). He is a specialist in the use of case study to portray and understand educational settings. Though his work leads him to observe many areas of professional practice (schools, police training, civil rights etc), he has spent much of the past five years conducting sponsored enquiries in the performing arts and education.

Acknowledgements

The research for this report relied heavily on the collaboration and on the tolerance of the City of Birmingham Symphony Orchestra and the teachers in the Birmingham schools I visited. In particular I should mention Sarah Scott, Education Officer of the Orchestra who looked after me on my visits, negotiated my way and gave me many insights into the working of the Adopt-a-Player Scheme.

Thanks, too, to the Birmingham Education Authority and to Linda Gilbert, Music Adviser.

The Calouste Gulbenkian Foundation provided the funds and negotiated the commission with the Birmingham Education Authority and the City of Birmingham Symphony Orchestra. Thanks to the Assistant Director for Education at the Gulbenkian, Simon Richey, in particular, for his help in arriving at a final draft, and for encouraging me to take risks.

All the names of schools, teachers and children in this account have been altered.

i

Foreword

In 1987 the Gulbenkian Foundation grant-aided the City of Birmingham Symphony Orchestra so that it might further develop its educational work in primary schools. The vehicle for this was the so-called 'Adopt-a-Player Scheme', a project devised in collaboration with the Birmingham Local Education Authority, which made it possible for individual players to pay regular visits to local schools and to work closely with the children. The scheme was part of a growing move among orchestras to develop more coherent programmes of work for schools and community groups.

Because such developments were still relatively new, and because a book had yet to be written about the relationship between schools and orchestras, the Foundation decided that a publication might prove timely. When Saville Kushner was commissioned to write the book in question, it seemed to us that the educational work of the CBSO might be a suitable medium through which issues potentially relevant to a greater number of orchestras and schools could be explored. This last point perhaps needs emphasising lest readers expect to find here no more than a formal evaluation of the Adopt-a-Player Scheme. The book has a different purpose.

The approach the author adopts is unorthodox in that he considers his subject less from the conventional standpoint of a detached observer than from the perspective of the participating children. What does a visiting orchestral player mean to them? What place does such an event occupy in their own cultural worlds? From there he goes on to look at the ways in which teachers and players perceive such initiatives. How the different parts of this cultural jigsaw fit together, and the nature of the educational activities that emerge as a result of it, is what the book wishes to convey. It offers no simple prescriptions or solutions. It respects the often unpredictable and elusive interactions between performing musicians, teachers and children and observes and reflects upon what the author describes as 'the complexities that these interactions encapsulate '.

We hope that this book will afford some insight into those complexities and, as schools and orchestras increasingly come to recognise the value of working together, prove thought-provoking and stimulating to teachers and players alike.

Simon Richey
Assistant Director, Education
Calouste Gulbenkian Foundation, UK Branch

Contents

Introduction

School curriculum is being nationalised, the high arts institutions are being forcibly 'opted out' from the system of public subsidy, and a child in a primary school imagines her grave will get narrower as a punishment for singing. Meanwhile, children work alone in a classroom, arguing, joking and, finally, composing a piece of music together. Their teachers sit upstairs at lunch and laugh about receiving a message of sympathy from their counterparts in Chile, and, on the other side of Birmingham, hearing-impaired children rehearse a piece of music theatre they will perform to other schools, passing silent meaningful looks to each other. Salman Rushdie is in hiding and Muslim children in another primary school wrestle with the issue of his right to live. An orchestral musician sits in the stalls of an empty concert hall speaking indignantly of the impoverished state of inner city schools... This is part of the stuff of the Adopt-a-Player Scheme - the educational programme of the City of Birmingham Symphony Orchestra (CBSO). In this thumbnail sketch there are traces of politics, culture, prejudice, professionalism, confusion, hope and exasperation, and it is of these that you will read in this account.

Such a mélange is no longer uncommon in research - though it is still not present sufficiently to portray our real experience of arts and education. This is after all about schools, and schools, while ostensibly preoccupied with teaching and learning, are social places. Society spills over into schools and the learning that goes on cannot ignore it - even if our prescribed school curriculum increasingly tries to do so.

The aim of this account is to understand something of the educational impact of this music-in-education scheme, perhaps to learn something for other such activities. It is based on brief but intensive bursts of fieldwork - and 'naturalistic evaluation', as it is known in my trade. 'Naturalistic' in that it tries to portray thoughts and events as they are experienced; 'evaluation' in that it puts enquiry to the service of better understandings of how our resources might be used. *"We need to portray complexity,"* argued Stake (1), a leading advocate of such approaches to evaluation. *"We need to convey holistic impression, the mood, even the mystery of the experience."*

For those who have read a Gulbenkian report which precedes this one - Paul Willis's *Moving Culture* - this one offers a contrast. In that report Willis acted as a kind of reporter - going out there and re-counting what he found. You read of young people's values, needs and dilemmas through his words. Here, you encounter children's words and actions in a more direct way and you have to do some of the work in making sense of them - insofar as I, the writer, allow for that.

But what of the Adopt-a-Player Scheme? This music-in-education scheme is conceived and carried out as a collaboration between the CBSO and the Birmingham LEA (Local Education Authority) - aimed at supporting teachers to develop skills in using music in (and across) the school curriculum. It is one element in the picture of what is happening in schools and the arts throughout the country. Many performing arts groups have education programmes like this one - indeed, arts groups in receipt of public subsidy are usually required to do this kind of work as a condition of the grant. There is a sustainable argument which says that current innovation in the arts is at least as much to do with where and how the art form is practised as with its actual content (though that changes as a result). Artists increasingly find themselves in unfamiliar places. The CBSO players are among them.

There is, however, little interaction between the Adopt-a-Player Scheme and other music outreach schemes taking place elsewhere. It is a localised initiative, as unique on its own patch as others elsewhere - it probably makes comparable errors, develops comparable understandings and scores equivalent successes. The Adopt-a-Player Scheme breathes the same cultural 'air' as those other arts initiatives, so it should come as no surprise that much of its rhetoric is similar, as are many of its working practices. It is not the same thing as the Guildhall Ensemble or the Royal Opera House Education Programme or the Liverpool Philharmonic schools programme or the Firebird Trust or Community Music - but they are familial.

These initiatives are potentially exciting - some of the country's musical élite working face-to-face with children. In many ways they reflect the aspirations of the Gulbenkian Report (2) which is so widely read by artists and educators. We will see the Adopt-a-Player Scheme, for example, reaching for the six aims for the arts in schools outlined in that report: developing the full variety of human intelligence and the ability for creative thought and action, educating feeling and sensibility, exploring values, understanding cultural change and difference, and developing physical and perceptual skills.

The major theme of that report was that the arts should be protected from the harsh demands of the new accountability culture in education - given the freedom to thrive in their own terms and to offer nourishment to other parts of the curriculum. This would be achieved through innovation - exploiting new opportunities - and innovation was something that people would conceive of and do themselves.

But reading the Gulbenkian Report at the gateway to the 1990s can produce an uncomfortable feeling. The expansionist and collectivist values underpinning that report (recommending a redundant college of education be set aside for training youth and community arts workers) feel somehow misplaced in the modern political economy. The vision of a thriving, integrated, resourced, varied curriculum for the arts looks like a hollow optimism up against the monolithic National Curriculum and the educational 'bully-boy' of national testing. The reality of the 1990s is that innovation is not so much something people choose to do - but something they are generally required to do.

The Adopt-a-Player Scheme is, however, one of those innovatory projects that stems, largely, from choice. In that sense it harks back; it also has a familial tie with the world of the Gulbenkian Report. The Scheme is small in scale, unambitious, unashamedly local in an epoch of grandiose national innovations. It is manageable, and it grows out of what each individual can put into it.

The Gulbenkian Report, too, specifically called for evaluation of schemes which bring professional artists into contact with school children - *"methods of evaluation applied to these schemes must reflect the nature of the processes involved".* The Gulbenkian Foundation's commissioning of this report on the Adopt-a-Player Scheme falls in with that recommendation. The Report argued that evaluation of the arts be *"illuminative"*, looking at *"actual effects"*, portraying the *"quality of experience"* and acknowledging values and *"intuition"*.

This account tries to be positive whilst retaining a critical and independent view - approving, that is, but questioning. It is just one of the stories that could be told of this Scheme and a pretty higgledy-piggledy one at that. Here it portrays children working, then it switches to teachers talking, back to the children and then to the CBSO players - and all the time referring to the process of doing this enquiry. But that's the way these things happen and it is the way people experience them. It is an attempt to see adult plans and initiatives through pupils' eyes and in pupils' terms. This is not an easy thing to achieve in research and the difficulty of capturing it is reflected in the difficulty of putting neat frames around things. To the adult eye the child's world is a sprawling, often poorly organised one in which conventions and tolerances may easily be overstepped. To the extent that this is true, this account may have 'gone native'.

Children, teachers and musicians explore sounds and music on the 'Adopt-a-Player' scheme (Pages 6-9) *All photographs by David Bent except page 7 top and bottom which are by Anne Baird*

9

I. Children in School

Richard is a slim boy of 10 in a blue-check shirt and slightly faded blue jeans. He has fair, red hair and a thin face with freckles. He has something of a distant look in his eye - a nervous, perhaps wary look. He's quick to break into a smile, but it's tight. He sits on the edge of the group his hands held at chest height and, suspended from them, Chinese bells poised one above the other like a two-piece mobile.

There are half-a-dozen 9 or 10 year-old children in the music room with an orchestral player. Richard concentrates on the bells, his hands still, but not stiff. Sitting on the floor in front of him are four other boys, all playing glockenspiels or xylophones, animatedly looking across at each other, shouting instructions with stern facial expressions, smiling, or else putting on that blank face that belies concentration. One of the four runs his beater up and down his xylophone languidly and in apparent boredom. Richard releases one hand, the higher one, to fall in a precise line allowing one bell to strike against the other. He raises his head - keeping his body and hands in the same position - to look at the rest of the group. He looks back at the bells and repeats the gesture and the sound, and again, and again. One of the group raises a hand, limply, as though it had suddenly become weightless, and everyone stops playing - momentarily - then they follow the boy who looks bored into the next section of the piece. Richard strikes the bells again. The music continues, and at the urgent signals of Lee the instruments drop out one-by-one, himself included. Then there's just Richard. He sits, almost hunched now over the bells and, to end the piece, strikes them five times, growing quieter each time, until the last one is barely audible. A flicker of a smile crosses his face as his shoulders drop. The boy sitting on the floor immediately in front of him brings a fist crashing down on Richard's foot and laughs.

At break-time the whole primary school is out in the playground in the hot sun. The scene is familiar, has been for years. Ball games, games of tag, huddles, arguments, hints of sexuality, screams and unheard whispers - a hubbub. Richard leans against the wall, his eyes narrowed against the sun, and watches it alone. He pushes his hands against the wall and his body jerks forward. He spins round, reaches up, grasps a section of drainpipe and pulls himself up to look into it, his feet scratching for a hold on the brick wall. He lets himself fall, turns again and leans back on the wall, folds his arms, unfolds them and looks down at his feet. He looks across the playground again. No-one runs past him. Children stand or play in discreet groups like chess-pieces confined to squares.

Richard relates to other boys in his class through a combination of banter and victimisation. *"He's a scientist!"* his mates laugh tauntingly - a child can become an object of mockery for displaying scholarly detachment. But it's more complex than that, in a way that's difficult to work out, even by talking to Richard and his mates.

Now he's standing just inside the door to the playground - hovering in a moment of uncertainty. As I approach him and start to talk, two of his mates move in closer, bouncing tennis balls off the wall and laughing and chatting, muscling in on the conversation.

"Why are you playing the Chinese bells?"

"'Cos I came to the group late and they'd all chosen the instruments."

But he likes the music - it's their own music, he says. Sure, Lesley comes in from the CBSO but *"she told us when we was playing too high or too low"*. *"Yeh"* bursts in John ricocheting a ball off the wall. *"She says when it's a bad sound!"*

"But it's still our music," says Richard. And the conversation turns more generally to the school.

"Yeh - it's a good school. Better than Banes," Richard accuses. *"My sister went there for about two years and she knows nothing. I know more than her and she's four years older than me!"*

But John insists that it's not as good a school as one which allows you to come *"when you want to"*. Richard agrees, thinks a moment and approves of the notion of a voluntary school.

"Yeh - you should come whenever you want to," he says.

"Every 5 weeks!" shouts John, catching his ball again, laughing. Richard is not laughing though. John bounces his ball and lurches into Richard

exaggeratedly to catch it, and Richard topples for a moment.

"You could come one week," speculates Richard, *"and take the next week off."* But John presses and taunts and continues to knock school. Richard looks at him and laughs and then *"Yeh! Just think! Come in school just for break-time!".* But he manages to make it clear that he does like school. So it's worth chancing one of those zoological questions that are easier to ask than answer.

"So what's it like to be a pupil?"

Richard kicks an imaginary stone with his foot. *"I don't know. I ain't never been a teacher."*

But teachers - researchers, too - have been pupils, though it doesn't guarantee our capacity to understand the world of the child in today's school. To the observer, Richard has the bearing of one who suffers relentless predation from his peers. But he can still laugh with his tormentors and they can suspend their bullying for long enough to share the humour - and Richard can create with them the brief moment of gentle concentration we saw at the opening of this piece. The logic of children's action and the working of their tolerances may be different from those of the adult, and in ways they do not freely talk about - it's hard to discover through the blunt instruments of observation and questioning.

This is not rhetorical. What it means for teachers is that, in a very practical sense, they can school children and teach them, but they cannot always be sure when and how they are educating them. The legacy of lavish resources and political favours given communities of educational psychologists over the course of this century has produced only conjecture and controversy over the basic question - how do children learn? In education, teachers often have to rest content with being an audience to children and with treating curriculum as a set of hopes and experiments rather than certain enterprises.(3)

Lesley, one of the CBSO players, notices Richard in his precarious place in the pecking order - and she doesn't like that. There had been a bid by one of the boys in his group to end their musical piece with a xylophone and not with Richard's bells. Richard looked on without saying anything as the boy tried to justify it musically. Lesley resisted - made one of those teacherly decisions. *"He does really concentrate on those Chinese bells."*

What this says is that teachers' plans and actions may often be filtered through a clash of logics. In the end, serious attempts at designing, developing and delivering curriculum, end up as attempts at drawing closer to the way children think and act - the National Curriculum notwithstanding. Teaching, we might say, is as much a matter of negotiation as it is one of transmission. Indeed, many modern curriculum theorists argue that a curriculum which aims to educate (rather, say, than simply train in specific skills) is based on a relationship between a teacher and a pupil of mutual dependence.

There is a version of that, offered by Basil Bernstein (1970) in his sociologist's view of school curriculum - a way of putting it which may resonate with the experience of artists working in schools. When a child steps into school, he says, she steps out of ordinary experience and temporarily loses links with life *"outside".* That, he says, cannot be ignored by teachers who have to be able to bridge that *"reality gap".* But how to do it? *"If the culture of the teacher,"* he argues, *"is to become part of the consciousness of the child, the culture of the child must first be in the consciousness of the teacher."*

That is where this report will begin and end. Bringing culture into consciousness. We will look at educational (ie learning) interactions between performing musicians (from the CBSO), teachers and children and how involved and intricate these interactions can be. This touches on the work of many in that family of performing musicians working in schools. Certain skills and understandings have developed quickly among them - their work has even begun to generate its own orthodoxies and some may be recognised in this account. There are even hopes that such work may displace traditional music education.

But there is a basic problem that still has to be addressed. The traditions, the practices and the values of orchestras and opera companies grow out of the professional culture of music and the performing arts. Schools which performing musicians visit have a different history and a different professional culture. Whilst competent to judge the quality of their own artistic practices, how do performing musicians judge the quality of their education work - because here the measures of what is good and worthwhile grow out of different problems and values?

Is something that is good musically, necessarily good educationally?

This is a question of educational quality, and to begin to address it we will look closely at children. We will listen to children talking and watch them in action and in interaction. We will do that before we look directly at the Adopt-a-Player Scheme (AaPS). Later we will look at the Scheme's impact on teachers and musicians - those on the other side of the cultural 'gap' from children, and we will see that the Scheme can stimulate professional development in both - it can be educational for children, players and teachers.

How do we go about looking at these events?

This is an increasingly common concern in the arts and education as people are asked to evaluate what they do, or as they choose to evaluate themselves to forestall a more unpredictable evaluation from somewhere else.

The reader can use this account to look into the AaPS, but also to look into the research process. There is, I hope, a transparency to this account, to allow the reader to see beyond the events being depicted to the production process behind it. The faltering interview shows up the hopping from classroom to teacher to child to player in an attempt to weave together different stories, the slow rumination that eventually leads up to some kinds of understanding. The following observation, for example, is interrupted by an interview with Leora, a teacher - here begins the 'messiness' I mentioned at the end of the Introduction.

There are important questions to ask about the research process as much as about the AaPS. Do the flaws and idiosyncrasies of the research process add to our problems of understanding children - or reduce them? What do we need to know to arrive at some understandings about the children and their relationship with music?

These are questions about what we include in our research and how we include it. (This research account uses narrative, direct observation, personal portrayal, photography...) There are also questions to be asked about who does the research and what difference that makes. I am an educationalist, not an artist - if those categories make sense. So it is not surprising that I seek out schools and children.

Ready!

We are in Rose Lane School. Inner urban, a community under stress (say the teachers), an old, poorly furnished red-brick building but with the brightness and buoyancy we are accustomed to in English primary schools. There is no music specialist in this school - the Scheme is challenging teachers' as well as children's capacities to work with music.

The children - 8 to 10 year-olds - are in the music room unaccompanied by their teacher. They are expecting Miriam from the CBSO to come in later in the morning. For now their teacher has left them with an exercise: she pops in from time to time to see how they are coming along and to encourage them to experiment. A jungle-type sound, you might say, is being played: hollow wooden blocks give a resonant 'woody' tone; a drum beats softly and repetitively; a triangle tingles; and a whistle gives bird-like 'whoops'. Against the drabness of the classroom the music creates an atmosphere. Children are playing these percussion instruments - they have no teacher with them. The music builds up in intensity and the children bok and ting with blank and even bored looks on their faces. The music is improvised but orchestrated. The music stops as the drum bangs an emphatic end, catching one girl by surprise.

"What are you doing? The music's supposed to be fading out!"

"Andrew wasn't paying attention."

"I was," says Andrew defensively. There is silence for a moment. *"Who do you think you are - teacher?!"*

"I'm me," the girl shoots back accusingly. *"The question is, who do you think you are?"*

"Come on," says Andrew, *"let's do it again."*

"I'm doing it," as one tries snatching a beater from another's hand.

"No, I'm doing it!"

"Ready!"

They play again. This time the piece is soft and rhythmic with regular pulsations on xylophones giving it an almost hypnotic quality.

"Why didn't you come in?" one girl shouts accusingly.

"You should have said."

"I did!"

An argument ensues as one or two scrape or bok their instruments loudly rather than join in.

"Shelley can sit on there 'cos she's the oldest."

"I'm not - Richard's the oldest."

'I'm older than Richard - and I'm older than Anthony!"

"Ready!"

They slide into another variation of their improvisation - again it has a slightly different quality - faster, more frenetic. It finishes abruptly and just as abruptly the argument begins again. A new shout of *"ready!"* and they play again.

This time the music has a dynamic quality as it goes from a loud pulsating phase into a tranquil section with the transition marked by a tapping cymbal. It is a spontaneous shift to which everyone responds even though some are not happy to do so.

"What are you doing?"

"Fading."

"You shouldn't! You should stop and start and - " as this voice is drowned out by the noise and the echo.

The teacher, Leora, walks in amid the hullabaloo.

"Have you started sorting it out?"

"We're still figuring out the ending."

There is some half-hearted attempt to explain to her as she kneels down patiently listening.

"So how are you going to make it fade away?"

One or two explain in a way that bears only small resemblance to what they actually played before she came in.

"And if you're fading out for the ending are you fading in for the introduction...have you tried different ways of starting?"

"Yes, Miss. This sounds best, Miss."

"That sounds best? Okay. Have you decided whether you're playing all together?"

"Yes, Miss."

"Are you using metal and wood together or are you using metal and wood separately or what?"

Voices are muted, now, and one or two mumble replies.

"You've worked all that out?"

"Yes, Miss."

"So once you've got the ending sorted out we can record it and then have a listen to it? Okay?"

They ask how long it should be and she tells them to make it as long as they want.

"I wouldn't have it too short, though, otherwise people will be getting just tuned into it and then it's gone. Try to make it fairly long. You know what you're trying to show in the music - what's Puck actually doing in the music?"

They become excited, now, and start imagining the scene.

"Because he's creeping up to Bottom - to change his head - are you putting any of Bottom in the music at all? You remember when we listened to the overture - what did we hear in the overture?"

They agree that they heard an evocation of the donkey in the overture and they set to, trying to identify an instrument that might represent the donkey for them.

Suggestions fly out. But the teacher wants to steer them to something they hadn't thought of.

"No - it's not a made instrument."

And she finally reveals the instrument to be the voice. There is no surprise among the group and the teacher doesn't seem to expect any. She leaves them alone again amid a renewed clamour and says she'll be back in a few minutes. One of the boys turns round to ask me if I am a school governor.

Leora, in her forties, is an experienced teacher. She has an easy and confident relationship with her pupils. We have seen that she is happy to leave the children to themselves, and then to question them about the decisions they are making, pushing them a stage further on in their enquiry. For her, the AaPS was a frightening prospect, as it was for all teachers in a school which has no music specialist, and it was an act of courage to attend the initial meeting at the Town Hall. But since then they have learned to work with the Scheme, using it to catalyse cross-curriculum activities. Leora is speaking:

"Well our inner city kids...the children in this school generally need to be taught to ask questions. During the music process when they're composing with, obviously, a teacher's input as well, they will ask each other, 'do you

think that's right, or should you come in here, or should you go in there, or why are you doing that?' - which then leads on to the questioning process across the curriculum."

Does it?

"Oh yes - certainly leads to discussion between them. It definitely leads to cooperation in groups."

Miriam, the CBSO player 'adopted' by this school, stands talking with us and says that she was amazed at how musically productive had been the group of children she had just observed. Leora goes on to say that she notices children listening more to each other. They argue, she says, but that falls away after a few weeks. They begin to question each other. Critically?

"Oh yes. It's when they're questioning each other in the group it will be, 'do you think we ought to have a theme that's running through it?' or 'should we play this loud or soft - high or low?' - erm - 'should we repeat it?' 'which instruments sound best together?' - so it's all that sort of questioning that you teach them to ask themselves."

Does that produce pressure on you to adapt other kinds of teaching that you do? If you're teaching division, for example.

"That's a very good example, actually. There's more than one way of getting the right answer..."

Leora is too experienced and sceptical a teacher not to take that claim seriously. So I ask again about ceding control of 'right' and 'wrong'.

"I mean you don't say to children this is right and this is wrong, unless, perhaps, on moral decisions, and then it's questionable. But it's sort of, 'well which do you think is the best way to do it - could you have done it differently?'. Or 'could you even have presented your work differently? Does it have to be writing - could it be pictures? Could it be music?' "

So that's an approach you would use anyway - the music simply encourages.

"The music is a starting point for getting that through other subject areas - once they've got into the habit of doing it, we find that music is the best opportunity for getting into that habit. We did the 'Adopt-a-Player' last year, and the difference in - well, I suppose my teaching style and the learning style of the kids has changed because of that."

The conversation moves along, echoing in this classroom as we hover at the door. The echo is a reminder that classrooms are places for children - incomplete without the bodies and sounds that soak up the echoes. Teacher, evaluator, orchestral player - we share a common memory of life 'down there', and it is readily evoked when the children noisily re-enter the room to re-occupy it. I don't recall seeing an evaluator in my classroom at school, so I'm not sure how to see myself here and I easily feel rather out of place - easily thrown by questions as the children try to place me.

The conversation continues, but in another direction from the emerging view of a critical teaching approach. Miriam talks of how important the Scheme is in raising questions for orchestral players, too. *"We can be totally distant from anybody else,"* she says.

The class continues developing the piece, using the suggestions from their teacher and including a sung 'hee-haw' to represent the donkey.

"No wonder it's too short - you should let us play for a bit and then come in!"

"She told me to come in after them, too!"

"I didn't. I couldn't - no"

"You said come in after Karen -"

"She - she!"

"Alright - I come in about 10 seconds after Karen."

"Let Dustin do it then, and see how stupid it's going to sound!"

Silence.

"You're stupid - you just know it's going to go wrong - that's why you just want to show me up."

And they play.

One of the girls, a black girl, sits in the middle of the group playing a xylophone. Across the floor from her sits a boy playing an African shaker, sucking the end of the handle between repetitions of the piece. She leans over and tells him in an elderly-sisterly fashion,

"Take that out of your mouth - it's not good for you."

He does, and puts on a sheepish look. He rattles the instrument, adding to the general mêlée. Another girl looks up at him and says sharply,

"Don't keep rattling that - it gives me a headache,"...but immediately smiles as though suddenly noticing herself taking on adult airs.

The black girl watches the boy who is a thin frail-looking child, quiet and, apparently, not fully engaged, though he plays his part. The black girl is a prominent member of the group, physically large and confident in her personality. She fluctuates between enthusiasm for the music and apparent boredom. She sits there lackadaisically tapping her xylophone, hitting the bars from underneath. She is, herself, admonished by the boy playing the African shaker so she sits up and begins playing more positively. The group decides they are ready to play for the teacher and one of them sends someone to fetch her. A girl makes a sardonic comment to the boy on the shaker.

"I like your socks, they're very nice."

He looks down at his rather shabby mauve socks with embarrassment as the rest of the group giggle.

"Ah - leave him alone!" orders the black girl in his defence. *"At least he's got on a school uniform better than yours anyway. He's got the right colour."*

It is halfway through the session and their teacher comes in with Miriam from the CBSO. The teacher watches as Miriam sits facing the children who have all fallen silent.

"What are you going to play music about?" Miriam asks them.

"Puck."

"Puck."

"Yeh."

"Can you tell me something about him?"

"Well - "

"He's a goblin."

And they all clamour again to have their say.

"Can you - wait a minute. One at a time. Can you tell me about him?"

"Well, he's a mischief worker, and he's a goblin - and he turns Bottom's head into a donkey head."

"Really? Anything else?"

But the teacher knows what they know and she prompts them to say more about Titania and potions.

"Okay then," says Miriam, "let's hear the music."

They play.

"That's very good! Are you making the sound of a donkey, you two?"

"Yeh."

"Well, can you say it a bit louder 'cos I can hardly hear it. It sounds like a baby donkey. It's very good. Can you play it to me again?"

One looks at the other and giggles as she tells her to start. They play again and Miriam congratulates them once more. She questions them some more and asks them to play another piece they have prepared. After a few minutes the group have lost their initial reticence; they are back into the style of argumentation and giving each other instructions.

Thinking about the Data

How do we begin to look at accounts like this? At this point we do not need a direction for our analysis to aim at - we simply need to find a way of thinking about these rather complex accounts. What do we notice, for example, when the class works alone?

Perhaps most obvious is the apparent harshness in the way children talk to each other, which suggests less mutual tolerance than adults generally feel comfortable with. The language the children use with each other is - at least to our ears - punitive, 'angular', recriminatory and competitive. We could even see a discontinuity with the music that emerges which (whether 'good' or 'bad') shows they have control over mood - the musical mood shifts deliberately - and they control it through cooperation.

This is not to say that competition does not spill over into the music. At the very beginning Andrew submits to the relentless attack of one of the girls and loses his chance to end the musical piece as he would like it - abruptly. And, musical moments are used as excuses to attack each other verbally. However, the stridency of the way they talk to each other is not carried over into the way they play music together which can be soft and gentle (if the reader accepts my word as the vicarious ear). Nor do we see evidence that success at producing genteel music 'gentles' the harshness of the way they appear to treat each other.

There seems, too, to be something arbitrary about the arguments and in the way the children compete. A girl may be attacked for what she has played, but the reason for the attack may not be so much musical as social. Decisions about endings and changes are thrown out with no apparent logical development. But at the same time there is little arbitrariness to the music, which holds on to its structure right through the rehearsal and even develops. So we might say - on this brief analysis - that there seems to be a discontinuity between verbal and musical interactions, but each can spill over into the other.

There are other things to notice, such as the versatile way the children interact. They can switch style and content spontaneously - perhaps most noticeably with their instant change in tone when an adult enters the room. We see a broad range of emotional expressions in the space of this short account - anger, humour, appreciation, caring - and an equally broad range of interactive strategies - cooperation, competition, challenge, negation, encouragement, acquiescence, consent and mimicry. There is even a theatrical element to the interactions - as when the girls find themselves playing 'teacher'.

This observation offers little of an obvious link between *order* and *productivity* in the classroom - something adults tend to value highly, though Leora is comfortable with leaving the class to do things in their own way. If there is disorder here there is also discipline - albeit hidden beneath apparently undisciplined acts.

But let us focus in a little and begin to look at how the AaPS fits in. The CBSO players have fewer choices than the teachers. They have to find a way of working directly with children. We will look a little closer in a moment at how Miriam works with these children, but we can set out some markers from this first observation. On her entrance, for example, the children fell quiet. Then they became - uncharacteristically - monosyllabic. They switched strategies to receive this new adult. They were quiet and even decorous until comfortable with her.

We notice, too, that Miriam - being reasonable and maybe even playing her own strategies and 'buying' her way in - offered approving judgments of the music which, apart from one moment when the children applauded each other, was a novel addition to the tone of the class. Hitherto the children had been critical and challenging to each other. Miriam, too, can offer critique, as she shows (*"it sounds like a baby donkey"*) but she dressed it in phrases of approval.

One way of summing up what we are seeing here is to think of the classroom as a constructed event - which is to say that the interactions we see are deliberate, designed, non-accidental. People have reasons for the things they say and for the way they act. In that case, the construction is clearly a product of all those who are present - including the observer, of course, who, at the very least, provides an audience for the children's theatre. The question, then, is who has the major influence and what are the working rules of the construction?

One possibility is that the children are the masters and mistresses of these interactions - forcing adults into negotiating strategies to work with them and adeptly bringing their own strategies to bear in a flexible way. One aim of this Scheme is to pass responsibility for music creation to children, so questions from the adults are ways for them to check how that is going. Adults - including the teacher who is known and liked by the children - ask them questions in order to get access to them. However we may also note that questioning by adults can be a subtle disciplinary device, reasserting quietness and order. Questioning demonstrates power and control.(4)

What we are doing here is looking in some detail at the common observation that performing musicians going into schools are crossing the threshold of one professional culture into another. What we see is that the 'professional culture' of the school is more complex than that title suggests - that in the classroom, the versatile, expressive members of that cultural setting are the children. Professional musicians in schools are, in a sense, strangers in a strange land, and they are constrained to act as such. Indeed, this account is written with no intention of 'laundering' that strangeness. These observations reveal disjunctures between children and adults in these creative enterprises - they may not explain them.(5)

There is no urgency in answering these questions - we simply have to be sure we are raising appropriate issues. So we can move on to look at this same group (actually on an earlier date) working with Miriam who is on her first visit and has, therefore, been 'adopted'.

A Player in Class

Miriam has been introduced to the class by the head teacher and left there. She starts by asking the children to spread themselves out a bit and tries to establish where they are at.

(**C** = Child **M** = Miriam)

C   *We haven't started yet...*

M   *This is the fairies music?*

C   *Yeh.*

M   *How do the fairies come into the story?*

C   *Don't know.*

There is the sound of bells jingling, but nothing else being played. There is silence between Miriam's questions.

M *You don't know? No-one really knows about what time of the story the fairies appear? Are they - just part of the background, or is it - are the fairies important in the story?*

There is some small discussion.

M *Okay then - well, have you composed any music so far?*

C *No - we only just come.*

M *You've only just come? Well, fairies - I mean - how would you describe fairies?*

The bells continue to be rung in the background. The children speak quietly - their voices are easily drowned - especially on a tape recorder.

C *Gentle, Miss.*

C *Very gently, yeh -*

C *- soft -*

M *- very soft. Well, the instruments you have - would you describe them as being soft instruments?*

One of the class taps a chime bar.

M *That's quite a good instrument - that sounds quite - airy, doesn't it, quite light. Er...*

The bells continue to ring out.

M *What about the triangle - do you think that's - er - what do you think?*

It is played and there is a pause.

M *Do you think that would be quite useful to use?* (Her voice rising at the end in a questioning inflexion.)

C *Yeh.*

The triangle sounds again and a wood block is tapped in the background.

M *What else - what else have you got?*

C *The bells.*

The bells play - legitimately, now. A child pulls a beater along a cymbal at the same time.

M *Okay, then - er. We'll try to work out who's going to play first.*

C *I am.*

M *Greg's going to play first. And then what happens after that?*

C *We don't know yet.*

C *We haven't sorted that out yet.*

M *Well, fairies - that's got to be quite light and airy - so - only I'm not going to tell you what to do. You have to decide for yourselves whether you're all going to play together - er - that could be like all the other fairies... then maybe you ought to have an instrument to show - like - the King and Queen of the fairies - so that people can recognise that's the King Fairy and that's the Queen Fairy - perhaps - you know - something like that.*

There is silence in the group and Miriam laughs to ease the tension.

M *What do you think? Who's going to have instruments for the King of the Fairies, then?*

One of the children makes a sign that amuses the rest of the group and they all laugh as he volunteers himself. "He's not got a - a - batter," accuses another boy. The boy makes a funny noise on his instrument and the whole group laughs with Miriam. Tension releases.

M *What about the Queen Fairy?*

C *I could be the Fairy.* (By now there are more instruments being tapped and struck.)

M *Well - well - you know, they could be like - you could have, like, the King and Queen Fairy walking and that sort of thing and all the other fairies behind - and so -*

- and one of the girls makes a suggestion which Miriam picks up on and the noise increases as they move towards a first try-out.

What we see from Miriam's teaching is a change of pace, a change of working practices, a change of style. Earlier, we saw that the logic of exchanges between the children was hidden - buried, somehow, beneath the surface of their exchanges. The rules and tolerances were implicit. With Miriam the logic is external, visible in the questions she asks - it is explicit. Her questions seek to order and to impose a logic on the music. She asks whether the triangle would be *"useful"* to use; fairies have *"airy music"*, kings and queens something different; there must be clear links between music and story.

This is partly because Miriam's interactions are task-orientated (that's her job), whereas childrens' exchanges were also about their relationships. This means, too, that there is more 'theatre' in childrens' exchanges - fuzzier lines between 'play' and 'work'. When Miriam takes over there is less variety - it looks more like work.(6) We may note, too, that to offer the lead to children does not always mean centring the values and the content of the curriculum around the children. It may have the subtle effect of asserting the 'teacher's' agenda and values.

We will move on to another set of observations - of a different player in another school. Lesley has done a few projects with the AaPS. The style of these observations is different, too. I have written them into a narrative, trying to make them easier to read. They carry more information (about the classroom, the outside, about the children) but more of the data are my selections and even interpretations - so there is also more that is hidden.

A Midsummer's Day

Horton School. Outside it is hot - very hot. We are in the best summer for 13 years. These children are practising music for *A Midsummer Night's Dream* and this is, in fact, midsummer's day. Lesley arrives in the staffroom saying that the leader of the orchestra is not likely to turn up to the school as expected. It is the first day of the rail strikes. It is lunch time and staff in this tiny staffroom are seated in armchairs that line the wall, with coffee tables in the middle. The conversation is not untypical of staffrooms and ranges from jokes about the morning's work and things the children have said to the threatening political clouds that hang over schools. LMS (Local Management of Schools) is a common theme. School culture is exposed here - like a beach when the tide's gone out.

Lesley (from the CBSO) and Heather (the class teacher) sit in one corner and discuss the day's work. The kids are to present an assembly next Wednesday based on what they've done here. Lesley will take each of the four groups in turn - just briefly - to run through the music they have developed. *"They've changed a lot since you last saw them,"* says Lesley to me, *"they've worked on their own and some of it's really quite good."*

What they have done in fact is to have listened to a tape of *A Midsummer Night's Dream* and identified four emotions - panic, sleep, mystery and marriage. Each of the four groups of children has taken one emotion and created a piece of music around it. Heather has written a narrative which the children will speak in turns and in which the four pieces of music are set. The narrative includes explanations of what the music is, the process by which it was created and parts of the Shakespearean story.

Lesley is in the music room, now, waiting for children to be sent from Heather's class. She arranges the piano and chairs in a crescent, checks the instruments. The first group enter and the session begins. They have about ten minutes.

The first group

Lesley leans against the piano talking to the boy who's sitting waiting to play.

Lesley *You're not going to be here next week, are you?*

Pupil *No.*

Lesley *Well, are you going to let Lee do the piano then?*

The boy shrugs and moves away and Lee takes up his position at the piano.

Lesley *Do you know how it goes?*

Pupil *No.*

Lesley looks at the first boy and suggests *"Why don't you do it whilst I show him"* and the group, having all taken up their seats with their appropriate instruments, move into the piece they have created. There is a piano, a boy on a snare drum and high-hat, another on bongos, one on a wood block and a glockenspiel. The piece lasts about 30 seconds and involves a persistent, pulsating rhythm accentuated by pairs of quavers played on the piano (two fingers), starting at the lower end of the keyboard and working up to the higher end, increasing the volume and intensity. They start again. Lesley stops them.

"Listen to the rhythm and try to keep it even. It's almost like playing a drum," she says to the pianist banging her hands systematically on the top of the piano. *"You've got to keep the rhythm going very evenly - try starting quietly until you get up here* (pointing two thirds of the way up the keyboard) *then start getting louder."*

They re-start. The boy with the snare and high-hat plays the same quaver pattern as the piano, accenting every fourth. The piano plays a relentless ostinato while the glockenspiel plays a little rhythmic melody made up of crotchet-crotchet-triplet-crotchet. Lesley stops them again and talks to the pianist who still cannot sustain consistent rhythm. *"Keep the movement going - don't think about anything else."* She starts them off again but stops him again as he breaks down on the piano. *"Why are you jumping notes? It's the same all the way up - you're trying to be clever about it! Okay, let's do it once more - we've got to get it right once."*

The pianist stands with his head bent looking down at the keyboard intently as his fingers punch notes. He doesn't play so confidently or competently as the boy who originally played the piano but who will not be there next week. Every few bars he hesitates and shuffles his body a half-step to the right to bring his fingers - his arms held stiffly at his side - into line with the next set of keys. By the time the piece has finished he has moved about three feet from one end of the piano to the other. As the piece finishes with a crash on the high-hat he looks up still holding his hands by his side and looks around as though re-surfacing.

Lesley asks if anyone else would like to have a go on the piano.

The boy who has been playing the glockenspiel puts up his hand. Lee takes over his beater. The original pianist, who is now sitting next to the piano on the bongos, leans over as the new boy arrives at the piano and tells him to use the left pedal. But the boy who has shifted from the piano is also uncertain about the glockenspiel. Lesley, having noticed that in his anxiety he repeats his melody too quickly, tells him to leave more space between his repeated lines. Mentioning this to him she recalls that she has to keep a record of which notes are to be used on the glockenspiel because the instrument will be used by another group. To make it simpler, children (and their teachers) often remove all the notes not being played in a particular piece. While Lesley is making her record the boy on the snare drum leans over and shows the boy now on the glockenspiel again what his notes are to be.

The second group

The first group have left and are now back in class and they have asked for the next bunch to be sent in. A solitary boy walks in and Lesley greets him. He replies with a subdued *"Hello"*. The others burst in chattering and laughing.

Lesley   *Okay - do you want to get your instruments out? Oh - you use one of these don't you?* (offering a beater)

Pupil   *Miss!*

Pupil   *Miss.*

Pupil   *Sonia! What letters do you use?*

Pupil   *You've given me the broken one!*

There is a quiet hubbub - music starts out in different parts of the room as children collect instruments (they are put back each time a group leaves), take up their position in a circle and start improvising. The previous group were all boys - this one is mixed.

Pupil   *There's one of these here!*

Lesley   *Oh, right. There's another blue one here, do you want a blue one?*

The blue one refers to two beaters which are more sensitive than the others and which Lesley generally prefers. Later she will spend ten minutes looking for them only to find they have been hidden away by pupils who have also discovered a preference for them.

Lesley   *Ready then?*

Pupil   *No.*

Lesley   *No?* (noticing the pupil fussing about with notes on a xylophone) *What notes have you got there?*

Pupil   *B, D and G.*

Lesley   *Right. Okay. What are we going to do about the beginning? How do we play this?*

Pupil   *It goes quiet - then soft - then louder - then soft again.*

Lesley   *Good, right - it's good to remember that shape - that'll help you to remember how to play it.*

They play. The boy playing the glockenspiel looks across at me with a sheepish but concentrated look. They finish.

Lesley   *Great! That was very atmospheric - it was really good.* (She, too, looks over at me.)

Again the piece lasts just 30 seconds but it moves through a number of moods. There is a tinkling piano, a percussive xylophone and a cymbal played with a circulating metal brush. A girl runs a beater up and down a glockenspiel.

These interactions are very different from the ones we saw at Rose Lane School. Here, there is a very tight definition of the working context in which music is to be played. Children work in their classroom until they are 'summoned' to the music room. Miriam walked into the children's self-styled set-up; here, the children join Lesley in 'her' room.

Each group is different, though Lesley appears to be comfortable with them all. Her style does not change and her role is consistent. She is aware of the social interactions taking place - the competitions, for example, and the pecking orders - and she has come to know the pupils well enough to call them by their names. There is a balance between the children's self-direction and direction from Lesley. She plays a kind of quality-control function. The approach is judicious, she is more concerned to get each piece right and presentable than to encourage adventures. She questions the children as encouragement.There are two more groups waiting to come in.

The third group

Lesley again is alone in the room for just a minute or two while the groups change over. Two of the 'cool kids' from the class stroll in with a rolling adult gait. They wear shorts in the modern psychedelic fashion, down to their knees and in fluorescent purples, greens, blues and reds. The two boys are talking bemusedly about another who is hesitating before coming in. Steve - the boy who appears to be one of the popular characters in the class - talks disingenuously as he wanders in a figure of eight saying *"For some reason he's afraid of us. I don't know why he should be afraid of us!"* but saying it in a way that suggests he does.

The boy they're talking about wanders in self-consciously. It is Richard, the boy we saw in the Introduction. He wears long, faded jeans and a check shirt. Within moments he is in the thick of a noisy mêlée - negotiating along with others to find the right instrument and beater. This group are all boys and they all, in fact, play a xylophone - apart from Richard who plays Chinese bells. As they are making their way to their chairs Steve accidently-on-purpose drops his xylophone on Richard's foot and laughs.

This group has many of the dominant characters of the class in it and Lesley has more trouble organising it. They are constantly shouting instructions to each other - more concerned than the others to manage their own affairs. Musically, the piece they play is also more complex than the previous two. One of the group raises his hand three times to signal a change of rhythm and mood.

Steve likes to take a prominent role and throughout the piece his eyes go all round the group, nodding his head, giving intense glares, trying to orchestrate. At the end of one run-through he turns round to one of the other boys on a xylophone *"That's out of tune"* he says. The boy checks and discovers that the damper is switched on deadening the sound - which is what Steve meant. He releases it. Lesley catches his attention *"Can you try playing with the other side of your beater? It sounds a bit brash"*. She looks around the rest of the group who have been discussing the piece. *"Is there anything else you're not happy with?"* Richard sets off to find another set of bells - *"These are rubbish!"* he says.

Between rehearsals of the piece there are discussions about how to improve both the piece and the way they move from one part to another within it. Lesley has odd conversations with individuals in the group and during these moments the rest experiment and practise. Richard leans forward and taps his bells on the xylophone. They play the piece again, this time with Steve pointing to make people drop out in turn. But his is a weak physical gesture, not noticed by two of the boys and he has to whisper to catch their attention. Lesley talks to him about this at the end of the piece trying to explain that if his physical gesture is confident, and the others responsive, he doesn't have to make a sound.

The fourth group

This final group are all girls. They are standing around the piano looking inside for the source of a rattling noise as though something is fouling some of the strings. One of the girls is Asian called Belinda and she says she's about to get a keyboard for her birthday - and a dog.

Belinda *And other things.*

Saville *What are you going to like best?*

Belinda *I don't know - the dog I expect.*

Saville *You're not getting a cymbal?!*

Belinda plays the cymbal in this piece - this was a weak joke.

Belinda *No, I don't like the cymbal. It's boring. And I don't like the noise - it's too much...music. Too loud. I don't like cymbals.*

Saville *So why play it?*

Belinda *I was doing my job and Gina wasn't doing it properly, so she made me do it. I was going to be in a different group. I was doing my job.*

Even so, Lesley keeps her at it - playing the cymbal. She talks to her about it between repetitions of the piece. Getting her to play it with subtlety, for example, to hold a pause for a fraction longer before giving the cymbal a regal crash after a piece of grandiose playing on the piano.

In this group, too, there are competitions and pecking orders and there are dominant girls. There are two Asian girls on the piano - one is tall, confident and imposing. She has piano lessons. Heather says they are more precocious than it appears and they stand slightly apart from the class, though not aloof. The music is built around them playing a duet on the piano. The others are required to drop out strategically during the piece while the two girls play the piano all the time loudly and with prominent melodies. Lesley confesses she is irritated by their dominance and by the less than competent playing. Belinda taps away relentlessly and faultlessly on her cymbal. She sits half-slumped in her chair, holding a drum stick in one hand and covering her face with the other.

We have seen something of the operation of the Scheme. We have been inside classrooms. Some of the complexities have begun to show through - particularly, perhaps, that cultural divide. We have also begun to see some of the style and practices of the AaPS and the mix of relationships it produces. Finally, I have tried to provide access to the research process.

The picture we have seen thus far is something of the view we may imagine children have of such projects. They get to see fragments of the total action - those fragments which involve them directly. It is from those fragmentary glimpses and from the explanations they are given that they infer the rationale.

But for our purposes we need now to look more broadly - at the context and at the rationale, and to understand something of the Scheme at different levels. We need to stand back to get an overview of the Scheme.

2. The Adopt-a-Player Scheme

What the Scheme is for depends on where you are standing.

From the point of view of the Birmingham Education Department the Scheme is an attempt to use the orchestra as an educational resource for city schools - specifically, to stimulate curriculum development. For the orchestra itself, the Scheme is an opportunity to *"develop an understanding and a bond...(and)...strengthen the links between the world of a professional musician and the world of a child"* (from the CBSO leaflet on the Scheme) and to go some way towards nurturing audiences of tomorrow.

For sponsors who put up the money, the AaPS is an opportunity to make a contribution to a social programme or else to publicise themselves. *"We just want to try to get across to people that we are interested in benefiting the communities that we're in,"* said one commercial sponsor. *"If that means that we do something to endorse what the CBSO have done and also to try and help fund it a little bit for them and try to integrate the children - then all the more suitable for us."*

For children, the project is an exciting addition to curriculum, a welcome break or a needless diversion from classroom tasks - or simply something that comes and goes with the many adults who pass through school. As we will see later, individual players and teachers have their own views on what the project is for.

In institutional terms, the AaPS takes professional musicians into work-spaces until recently guarded closely for and by teachers, who retained a monopoly on school education. The Scheme is a modern example of schools becoming more open institutions. It is, in some respects, revealing of an educational 'perestroika'.

The AaPS is many things to many people. It is something of a 'lucky bag'. In terms of outcomes, as we will see later, the Scheme has some impact in a number of ways - for teacher development, curriculum development, the professional development of the players. But we can say with greater certainty what it is that the Scheme actually does. It started in 1984 in about six schools as a result of an idea put to the chief executive of the CBSO by the LEA music adviser.

A concert is planned for, say, three months ahead - to play on this occasion, *A Midsummer Night's Dream*. From the players who will perform it, a small number of volunteers are chosen to take part in the AaPS. They will attend a meeting at which teachers from half-a-dozen selected schools will come to talk about the forthcoming term's work. Players will be partnered with schools (ie a school will 'adopt' a player), generally, one player, one school. A series of five visits will take place: each visit will be for a couple of hours, though players may stay longer - they usually do.

During the visits the players work with a teacher who may or may not be a music teacher. Children will be introduced to the concert piece, they will listen to tapes of the music, they meet and talk to the player and eventually they carry out workshop-based tasks associated with the concert theme. They will compose their own pieces of music with ideas stimulated by *A Midsummer Night's Dream*. The player will act as music 'animateur' and will spend time talking with the teacher about the childrens' compositions. The compositions will be played, perhaps at school assembly or to a special performance arranged for parents and other participating schools. The players also spend some time introducing children to the orchestra and to their instruments.

Towards the end of the term's project the children will go to the Town Hall to observe the orchestra rehearsing the chosen concert and, that night, they return to see the formal concert and to witness their 'adopted' player sitting on stage in formal dress. One intention is that an otherwise distant and impenetrable event is demystified as children watch the player in glamorous surroundings but are able to reflect on that player as they have known him or her.

In the meantime the collaborating teacher back in the school will have been using the visits of the players together with the concert theme to stimulate curriculum activities beyond music. The player might have spoken about touring - there may be geographical themes pursued as a result. Children will extend their musical imagination of, say, woodland scenes, into visual imaginings as painting. Instruments may be used to enter into science discussions based upon examination of sound. Or, in a more sophisticated way, there may be pedagogical elaborations - for example, using the music to demonstrate to children that the notion of 'right' and 'wrong' is a limited concept and that there are simply different ways of going about things.

But, in common with other social initiatives, this project lives in the minds of people as a set of values and hopes rooted in biographical memories. We can see this by focussing on one of the people who was instrumental in setting up the Scheme - listen to how she spoke about it.

The AaPS originated as an idea shared between the education authority and the orchestra - the prime mover was Linda Gilbert, the General Music Adviser to the LEA. Linda has a background in music education (and dance) in middle schools - trained in one of those pockets of the teacher-training world influenced by R S Peters, one of the progressive educational philosophers associated with the 1960/70s 'golden age' of curriculum reform. She was also taught by Peter Renshaw who is now one of the leading figures in bringing professional music-makers into interaction with communities. *"It was terrific groundwork,"* she says, *"I'm not a 'systems' person and I never was."* People, she says, share values, not views.

She retained from that phase beliefs which have never left her. At the core of these beliefs is respect for children as individuals and a theory of personal change. Children are to be treated as individuals with independent value systems, free to evaluate for themselves, free to make their own 'connections', encouraged to use music to think about themselves - not just to play music. Connections are important. *"How can you help that child to see what they've done in a wider musical context, in a wider cultural context, in a wider arts context, in a whole world context?"*

So music has to be interactive, based on one-to-one relationships. *"If the kids could get to know the player as a friend, then musically all sorts of things would happen."* Hence, schools would 'adopt' a player, invite a more intimate relationship than one in which the player was allocated to a school randomly.

Central to her view of individual change is the notion of 'sparking' a child - a momentary realisation, a condensation of experience, a catharsis. *"It may be just something internal, you may not even see it happen, you may have to work on a hunch, it might be a look in the eye..."* Such a concept is common enough in conversations with musicians - the 'moment' a person decided to become a musician. Linda talks of it in personal terms, recounting such a moment when she was dancing to a violin concerto - a life-changing moment. She clicks her fingers and narrows her eyes to describe its spontaneity and impact. A moment on a course when she felt she attained a level of expression hitherto denied her on her instrument. *"It was something intangible."* Her dance teacher came over to her and said he knew something had happened to her. *"It was probably the most moving experience of my life."*

There are many voices in this Scheme, each one with its own hopes and exhortations. We have heard, in depth, from just one and we have seen in it how this Scheme is an extension of learnings and experiences from an individual past. We will hear other voices as we move through this account and later we will hear from the players themselves. For now, we move back into the heartland of AaPS activities, but this time looking at it directly from the point of view of the children.

This next section is based on conversations with children and their teachers - sometimes talking in direct terms about the Scheme, other times talking obliquely about their experience and values. There is a persistent problem in research of creating realities that do not exist beyond the story being told. The very act of asking a question gives prominence to an issue that interests the research community and no-one else. If I ask someone's view about a music project they will generally reflect about it and try to answer. Had I not arrived they might never have given it a moment's thought.

We often, in research, imprison people within the confines of an overly narrow interpretation. We too easily see children as part of the story of an educational project, when it is at least as important to see how the educational project fits in as part of the story of a child's life. That inversion is rarely accomplished and I don't do it here, though the reader may see me trying to do it.

This often means not asking the question that is in my mind. I want to know if the AaPS features in the consciousness of children, and how - so I wait to see if they talk 'about' it (ie whether they share its concerns) and how they raise it. If a conversation passes without any reference, then that is, in itself, an important learning. Indeed, there is a reciprocal version of that - where I am over-anxious and cannot refrain from asking the question directly, and when we start hearing direct commentary on the Scheme, then we begin to doubt the authenticity of the research.

3. The Children and their Teachers

Hearndale School

Assembly is taking place. The packed hall is very large with wrought iron ornate arches, painted brick walls and parquet flooring. The sight is an impressive one, it looks like those old descriptions of mass meetings at the height of the Bolshevik Revolution. Almost all the children (and there are hundreds of them) packed into this hall and who are milling about in some theatrical performance are Asian. Many of the girls wear traditional dress in very bright colours - golds, blues, yellows, greens. The colours are reflected within decorations which hang on the walls and from the arches - tinsel, stars, streamers, gifts wrapped in paper. Most of the children are seated at the far end of the hall and the children who are performing (they number 30 or 40) are lined up along the far side and at this end where the teacher is leading them from behind the piano. On the near side there is a long line of gymnastic benches on which are seated a line of Asian women in sarees and some white teachers. There are children with face masks like rats, two have tall top hats made of cardboard. There is a lot of noise. This is a performance of *The Pied Piper*. *"I am the King of the Rats"* sing the children, with the teacher playing the piano and a group of children crowded together on a dais playing recorders. On the wall behind them there are posters and collages written in an Asian alphabet. This is the performance of a European folk tale but the festival being celebrated is Muslim - Eidmubarak.

Boy *I can sing Indian songs but not English songs, I don't like to sing them, I like to sing Indian songs.*

Girl *In our religion we're not meant to sing because it's a...'cause you get...I don't know how to say this because in our language you call it "G'nah" - it's a bad stuff.*

SK *If you sing in English?*

Few *Yeh.*

Boy *If you play instruments and things like that.*

Girl *No!*

Girl *Yes! You are allowed.*

Boy *If you sing in English it's not a good thing for Muslim children.*

Girl *Yes.*

Boy *And when you did, right, you get punished for it.*

Girl *No you don't!*

Boy *Yes you do!*

Boy *Yes you do!*

Boy *It's only that girls shouldn't sing and boys should because Mohammed did sing.*

Girl *No!*

It is, they explain, part of the final reckoning.

Girl *If you have more bad doings than good things - something like that...the grave goes really thin and this part goes...squeezed...and if you do good things, your grave it gets wider and wider...*

There are two CBSO players working in this school, Len and Maureen, and both are present today. The time after assembly is busy with music workshops which lead up to performances at the end of the morning. The players take two groups and teachers three others. Halfway through the two players are asked to talk to all the children involved - about 75 of them - about the orchestra. It is a stand-up presentation during which it is difficult to sustain the attention of so many children. But it is a test the players pass with a reasonable degree of success. There are some questions from the floor.

Girl *They say boys can do anything they want, what about the girls?!*

Boy *Stay in the kitchen!*

SK *What about playing an instrument? Are you allowed to play an instrument?*

Few *Yes.*

Girl *If the teacher isn't watching us we don't sing sometimes, but if the teacher is watching us we just move our mouths.*

The four children - two girls and two boys - sit and lie on the grass outside and in the shade of a tree. They are all Pakistani. Their English is very good. They question me closely about the book I am writing. Who will read it? How long will it be? Will it make them famous? Will it have pictures? There is a spontaneous competition to find a name and the one that I like is 'The Children's Music Book'. We talk a lot about music, but more about their religion, their view of school, relations between men and women. By the end of the interview they have independently raised the issue of Salman Rushdie and declared that they want to see him dead. But they pull back from that position. *"We are all going to die - no need to kill anyone."* Nothing, it seems, is sacred in their mouths.

SK *The music that you played this morning, what did you think about that music?*

C *I think it's good, spooky, spooky...*

C *I think it's rubbish. I didn't like it.*

SK *You didn't like that?*

C *Every week we do something different like music. We don't always do the same music.*

C *I like violin music. Kind of.*

That was one of the girls. What this transcript doesn't show is when a boy is talking and when a girl. Their responses are fired like bullets and off the tape it's hard to tell them apart. Also they keep lapsing into their own language to sort out their differences. They laugh a lot.

C *I like computer music!*

SK *Well, hang on a minute, tell me why you think it was rubbish.*

C *It was loud and spooky, I didn't like it.*

C *I like music.*

C *It was just a noise, bang, bang, bang. It was just a noise, it was not one instrument at a time. I didn't like it.*

C *It should have been one at a time. It shouldn't have been all banging so you don't know what they're doing.*

C *You don't know about what they're talking about in the story. You can't keep up with the story.*

SK *Alright, but you just said that the orchestra plays all of this.*

C *One instrument should make a different noise. That's good.*

There's something about the way that is said - "*that's good*". A closure, a certainty, a cultural equivalent to dogma. But they talk approvingly of the AaPS and of the efforts of the players. "*They teach us quite a lot,*" one says as others reiterate their dislike of music. Then all views coalesce as they talk about an aspect of school which they all like. Tests.

All *It's exciting.*

C *It's like a challenge.*

C *You have to find out the answer.*

C *You learn to solve problems.*

C *If you get all of them right -*

C *You get a bad if you get them wrong.*

C *So our teacher gives us team points.*

C *Team points.*

SK *Team points?*

All *Yes.*

C *We get badges the next day.*

Now the evaluator's antennae are out. Tests and collaborative music workshops - rhetorically, at least, are as far apart as might be imagined. Teachers in these schools frequently talk of the value of the AaPS in generating cooperation, respect for the views of others and an understanding that there are no 'right answers'. Tests are, by these children's account, at the other end of a spectrum. They are competitive, there are definite rights and wrongs and there are punishments. But they are, say the children with relish, *"peaceful"*. *"Everybody goes quiet - you have to tell everyone to go away...and it's very nice to have peace and quiet."* And this is in contrast to music which is noisy.

"We've been told the mould is safe as long as you don't breathe in the spores." A teacher is talking about the state of the school. *"You should come on a day when it's raining - buckets everywhere!"* Four of them sitting in a garret in the school - a poor room with minimal furniture, but a precious space where smokers can indulge. The 'smokers' room. The new floor has damp rising - the previous new floor was of concrete and had to be replaced because if gave off a dust that affected both teachers' and children's throats. By their account it's tough being a teacher under the new regime of national testing, national curriculum, high expectations of schools and reducing resources.

"We're getting letters from places like Chile saying 'very sorry to hear you have lost your negotiating rights'. That's ludicrous! They are writing to us!"

There is much laughter around these stark observations and you have to listen carefully to disentangle the despairing message from the buoyant medium. *"We're the poorest paid - the poorest respected - internationally,"* she says and laughs at herself as she shows how she lowers her head and mutters when asked to confess that she is a teacher in England.

The attacks come from all sides - including defenders of schools. An advisory team for maths came in recently on a 'visitation' and declared the maths department to be racist. *"They put us down as racists - I think mainly because we see our children as different."*

Most of the children in the school are Asian and there are major language problems - a variety of mother-tongues spoken at home and regular withdrawals of children to make home visits to Pakistan and India. The LEA employs no mother-tongue teachers in the school.

But the 'difference' can be put to effect. The authorities *("they")* are putting an emphasis on technical language and abbreviations in marketing national tests and curricula and this offers a subtle advantage to English-as-a-second-language children. *"Any word is a new word"* and they have as much chance of understanding 'polyhedron' as 'square' and some, according to this teacher, are already way ahead. But a colleague disagrees. *"I start my lessons by saying 'we're on attainment target 13, level 4...you will be able to represent, interpret and draw a diagram which will illustrate...' and by then you've got half the class going through their dictionaries."* She laughs and the others join with her - all nodding their heads in recognition. *"And all it means is they can draw a bar chart!"*

One of the four children, a boy, sits with legs crossed and fingertips pressed together and with a serious look on his face. He leans forward staring at the grass and plucks a blade to dissect it carefully as he listens and makes the occasional contribution. It is he who does not like music that is too noisy. *"Salman Rushdie calls himself a Muslim - but he isn't...you can say that Salman Rushdie is already dead."* His voice carries some authority in the group. The others clamour to talk and shout to be heard, whereas his voice tends to carry and assert itself. But he is shouted down by one of the girls who tries to explain that there should only be one integral god - contrary to Hindu belief in many deities and to Christian belief in Jesus. *"God's got no relations, got no parents...got no son...he's alone."*

But he listens, speaks infrequently - considers the question of whether killing really can be justified. Earlier in the conversation we had been talking about this publication and I had asked what might make the book exciting. *"Writing about different people!"* one had responded. My question had been prompted by one of them asking me *"Are you going to make it more exciting, the book, or just put words in that we say?"* He developed that.

"If you write about different people you can hear what they all think - can read what they all think. It's exciting."

"So if I write something - what you say - and then I write something that someone else says - "

"It's more exciting - the difference."

"Even if it makes arguments?" I ask.

"No! We don't want arguments!" one of the girls insists.

Back in the staffroom the teachers are making the best of a bad job - trying to persuade me to expose the hardships schools are having to go through in the modern age. *"Why are you doing this book - what's it for?!"* one asks accusingly. *"When are you going to present the results to the Tory Party to stop them banning everything artistic in schools!?"*

"Is that what they're doing?"

"Well, gradually the timetable has been reduced till we have very little time to do any of the arts at all."

Music came to the school when they acquired a music specialist teacher who is now the coordinator for the AaPS. Since then the children have taken a lead and one of these teachers explains that when it was her turn to prepare something musical for assembly she hesitated until the children told her to leave it to them. They had written a piece in the previous year and they could do it again. The male teacher in the room led one of the groups in the AaPS exercise this morning. *"Just think,"* he says, *"I'm not musical at all but you can get together with the kids and within a half-an-hour you can produce something that other people are going to clap..."* He is a maths teacher.

We sit and reflect on what school was like for us as children, and how I was encouraged to become enterprising. I remember spending so much time each year collecting jam jars to store in the air-raid shelter for some esoteric charitable purpose. They don't recall jam jars. Theirs are bottle tops. And newspapers. But that was dilettante stuff. This year the school has set up a 'mini-enterprise' which involves children running their own business. They sell orange squash to other children in the school. *"I'm making £10 a day,"* the supervising teacher laughs, *"they're making a huge profit!"* The children running the business elected a Board of Directors and they negotiated with the bank.

The profits are being used to buy cricket balls. Things are changing inside school walls.

The bell goes. The message from these teachers has been one of a relentless condemnation of the political condition of schools and teaching - spoken loudly and in good humour. *"A lot of us would be vocational teachers."* Are there any positive things to talk about, I ask, in Hearndale School.

"It's a wonderful school - everybody's happy here...the kids are great. The kids do really well when they leave!"

"So Thatcherism works? Starve schools and - "

"No. It's our kids. They want to learn."

Munkton School

Munkton School is across the other side of the city in leafy suburbs, reached by urban rail. We are sitting in the empty staffroom during lessons. I am sitting on an easy chair next to Ann, the music teacher - the girls (there are four of them) are sitting facing me on the floor. It is not comfortable, either because of the presence of a teacher or for the physical unease of looking down on these girls. I feel adult, important and detached - as though the authority of the teacher envelops me in their eyes. The conversation is hardly fluid. To start with, and in my own nervousness, I break my own rule about not asking the question I'm interested in.

SK *You've all been on this AaPS. What was it all about?*

G *We had a lady - a musician from the CBSO came in and played some music with us.*

SK *Is that what it was about? She came in and played music with you?*

They all laugh lightly.

G *Well, we listened to some tapes and we had to put our ideas of what* *we thought about in music...*

G *...we had to write poems and put them to music and - er - what else did we do?*

G *We went to the CBSO concert on the night -*

T *- and? Before that?*

G *- we went to a rehearsal.*

SK *Was it easy doing it - working with a musician?*

G *It was fun.*

G *Yeh.*

SK *Does that make it easy?*

G *Yeh.*

G *Yeh.*

SK *Does it? Can it be fun and hard at the same time?*

G *No.*

They laugh lightly again.

T *You don't think it's hard, do you, if it's fun?*

G *No.*

T *They actually produced some very very good work.*

The bare transcript belies a shaky opening to this conversation - too many hesitations and too much courtesy. But there is a spark of hope for a more authentic conversation than I feel is happening. One of the girls rejected my word *"easy"* and substituted *"fun"*, demonstrating some independence. The talk continues around the theme of poetry. But it runs out. I admit defeat and return to the question.

SK *Alright - alright - what about music, then? Playing music - is that something you did before?*

Murmurs of assent suggest a possible route here.

SK And - the music - has it changed at all since you've -

No need to finish - they seem to have predicted the question.

G Yeh *(in unison)*.

SK Why? 'Cos I asked you?!

G No.

SK How's it changed?

G Well, before we were just making sounds - now we're making a proper piece of music and writing it down rather than just using a tambourine and shaker to make noises - to create an atmosphere.

This answer sounds too good to be true and makes me feel even more exposed. I try to off-load my embarrassment on to the children.

SK That sounds like something that your teacher said, "creating an atmosphere", what do you mean, "creating an atmosphere"?

G Making the music like describe what you're doing it about.

Outside the sun shines very brightly and it is a hot day - one of the first of summer. These are the inner suburbs of Birmingham and the school campus has extensive playing fields. The staffroom has long windows and 'french windows' which give onto a patio and the fields beyond. A little earlier I had been talking to Ann about her experience of the AaPS and I had been excited by the conversation. She talked of how she had found herself learning alongside the children.

"I don't think I changed as quickly as a lot of people did - I came into the creative side relatively recently," she says. She had a formal music training and has always seen herself as not very creative. "I had to stop and think."

But what is the process of learning like for a teacher? Picking up skills? An intellectual exercise? "It's having someone to draw it out of *you,"* she says, something her 'adopted' player did for her. Then she can do it with the children. She gives an example. A document came with 'Images' - the theme for her AaPS project - which talked about how to analyse the music. It was helpful - but not so much as getting down and doing the work. She played the piece to the children with her collaborating player and the children gave a better analysis of it than she felt able to do.

"And understanding that their ideas were never wrong," she says, with enthusiasm now, "it didn't matter what they said. It could be right - just because it wasn't necessarily what Debussy meant in the piece - it was their idea, their feeling for the piece." And this was, too, when she started her learning. "We all started thinking more deeply - I started looking for more in the music and so did they." The search moved out into poetry and language, "they started to question and look all the time".

Back in the conversation with the girls the situation is no more comfortable. As I use the scissors-and-paste - weaving together the teacher's and the girls' accounts - it strikes me that I ought to have been thinking more of what the teacher had told me as I framed questions for the girls. But I was struggling to stay afloat, let alone think of what stroke I ought to be swimming. I put on a look of concentration and concern and turn to Ann...

SK *Hang on a minute - hang on a minute. Just let me pursue this - that alright? Er - tell me a bit about the kind of music that you - what's music? I know it's a stupid question -*

Everyone laughs out loud, this time. I have no idea where this question came from - or where it is supposed to go - it is a bid for freedom. I sit on a chair looming over the girls who all sit facing me on the floor and physically there is no way of righting the situation - so come down a level status-wise. People are still laughing.

SK *Well - these are things that we don't think about normally - you know what I mean - we just say - 'oh music (mumble)' - but you sounded like* *you were saying that now you play music but before you just made sounds - you know what I mean? And music's about creating an atmosphere - or - I mean - well, do you have to have an instrument to play music?*

They all say no.

G   *Voices - voices -*

SK   *Right - do you have to be singing to be making music?*

G   *No - no -*

T   *Think about the other two pieces you heard at the concert - especially the Boulez. The first piece.*

G   *Oh - the first piece - it didn't have, like, a harmony and didn't have a tune to it - was just like they were playing -*

G   *- just sounds -*

G   *- what they wanted to. We thought they were tuning up!*

G   *I know!*

SK   *You what?*

G   *We thought they were tuning! The teacher said they always tune up before they go on.*

SK   *Oh - I see! Tuning! Hah hah! What did it sound like to you?*

G   *A mess.*

SK   *Did it?*

G   *Yeh.*

SK   *Do you not like that sort of -*

G   *No.*

G   *No.*

T   *Some of the boys liked it, didn't they?*

G   *Gavin did.*

SK   *So you like things with tunes in -*

G   Yeh.

G   - if it's got good rhythm.

SK   Good rhythm - is that the kind of stuff that you play?

The girls are stuck for an answer - not sure whether their music is rhythmic or not. They spontaneously turn to the teacher who confirms that they use rhythm. They turn again to me and answer firmly and together "yes".

SK   Why did you ask the teacher?

They all laugh.

SK   No - why did you ask the teacher?

G   I don't know.

Talking of learning with Ann had spilled over into talking about the girls and what the AaPS had done for them. She was sure of the fact that learning had taken place - that the girls were different as a result - not just in what they could do, but different, too, in themselves. *"The confidence they gained - because of the sort of work - it suited everybody."* By this she meant the less able as well as the able. The Grade IV pianist came out less well than the girl with no formal musical training. Ann had been concerned to get the message across that there was no such thing as the 'wrong way' to go about things. *"They hadn't got to worry about the major grammatical constructions - points of a sentence, things like that...and although they altered a lot of what they did, it was because it felt right."*

Ann talks about the social effect of the Scheme - from the enthusiasm it generated - in showing the children how to work together. She experimented with various groupings and they all worked. But is there not an emerging contradiction with an approach that emphasises cooperation and the fact that there are no wrong ways of going about things? The National Curriculum is imminent and one critique has it that it encourages competition (particularly coming in tandem with national testing) and, under various political pressures, that there are fixed and absolute coordinates for knowledge. And music, anyway, carries a strong legacy of imperatives and rights and wrongs.

"I'd never say that to a child after singing Tippett's Mask of Time *the other weekend, when every note was being played at the same time. Nothing's wrong! If Tippet can do it and get away with it - they can do it. No - I think musically - I think in maths and language there are things that are wrong - but musically, no. I don't actually think there are things that are wrong. There are opinions."*

Have you been radicalised by this - is that a radical view of music?

"Possibly because I've been involved in a fair bit of modern music recently - like Tippett and Messiaen...there's feelings and things - no, I think a lot of music is opinion. It's what suits you. This is what I try to get over to the children - you won't all like the same things..."

The conversation with the girls has lurched into a discussion of how they have been learning to improvise - building on the work they started with the AaPS. What do they think improvisation is? *"Making a little tune on top of a piece of music,"* one says.

I repeat the phrase - to buy time but also out of habit - making sure that it is not lost on the tape-recorder.

G *A piece of music's being played and you, like, make a tune to go with it.*

They say they enjoy that. All laugh and Ann says she can't stop them now.

SK *Why - why do you like doing that? What is there about it?*

G *You can't make a mistake, really, can you?*

G *Yeh.*

G *You don't follow -*

G *- you don't particularly -*

G *- you're not following a piece of music that tells you you have to play this note on a certain beat of the bar, or something. You just play what you want to play.*

The interview continues for some ten minutes more and one of the avenues I try is to ask a question I often ask of myself - what do they feel as they prepare to go to school over breakfast in the morning? When the CBSO is coming, one says, she can't wait to get to school - unlike other days. Another disagrees.

SK *It's not the same for you?*

G *No, 'cos I'm in the orchestra and we do a lot of music.*

SK *And you play anyway.*

They all agree they do.

SK *You all play, anyway?*

G *Mmmm.*

G *Well...*(with some obvious hesitancy)

SK *Go on - what?*

G (Laughing) *Well I just play some stupid things.*

G *She plays the triangle!*

They all laugh as Ann says she is an *"unpitched percussion player"*.

SK *Why is a triangle stupid?*

They laugh.

G *All's you have to do is go 'ting'!*

They giggle uncontrollably.

We can begin to unpack this account - to find a way, once more, of standing back from it and making some analytic sense of it.

There is, clearly, a tension between the roles of the people in the conversation (researcher, teacher, pupil) and the kind of information that emerges. The question is not whether we believe the girl, for example, who says that she can't wait to get to school when the CBSO are there - or the whole group when they turn to their teacher before making an answer. The question is how we believe them. Is their personal view one that is repressed under the weight of their responsibility to act and respond as pupils? I was speaking strategically in response to the particular situation I found myself in - so why not the girls too? Indeed, the final interchange about the triangle seemed to show a more natural response, less clothed in the niceties, revealing of the authentic ways in which children talk to each other.

The question of whether people talk personally or are prompted by their role can be broadened a little. How can we be sure that people were not talking about the Scheme simply because I was asking about it? One of the effects of a formal enquiry into some activity is to bring that activity into a foreground that may, in terms of real experience, be uninhabited territory. The tendency of the girls to look to Ann for an answer to 'their' questions is a signal that they are looking for what might be expected of them. In the eyes of children, projects like the AaPS emerge from the adult world of institutions and roles, and in that world people are expected to speak in particular tongues.

There are aspects of independent thought throughout the interview, nonetheless. Perhaps one of the ways we judge that is to look for comments that pupils make irrespective of or in contradiction to those of their teacher. Here, the teacher speaks enthusiastically about her recent discovery that music has broader limits of tolerance than she had previously allowed. *"Nothing's wrong!"* And yet the girls take a different view - more conservative when listening to Boulez than the teacher had been when listening to Tippett; treating improvisation casually as an opportunity to relax discipline and to play 'wrong' notes legitimately.

There are less complicated stories in these observations, too. We hear from Ann evidence of how the AaPS stimulates her own professional development. She observes as well as works with the player: these are the beginnings of a professional development strategy, something like a 'modelling' process. The teacher has a bank of skills and understandings which require 'unlocking' - which the player helps to accomplish by example.

The process is more sophisticated than that, it is based on personal reflections and changes to herself. She has used the Scheme to re-examine her relationship to music, discovering new tolerances within her which feed back into her teaching. There is a cost to self-reflection - Ann has come to see herself (we do not need to take her word) as an uncreative person, but someone who can learn alongside her pupils. Indeed, in the interview Ann comes across as a more enthusiastic learner than her students.

Such observations are useful to us in acclimatising ourselves to the world of school and classroom; they sensitise us to those aspects of the educational culture which may not be familiar to those whose last contact with school was in childhood. What is professionally peculiar about schools is that children are conscripts and teachers have to balance custodial duties with emancipatory responsibilities. There are rules and routines which prevail in the spaces set aside for performing artists to work in. The classroom is not neutral territory.

Let us look more broadly at children in these schools. In the last account I noted an unfortunate error in opening a conversation with children with too direct an emphasis on the question I was asking. The result was to make me doubt the authenticity of the responses - I had provided them with too clear a guide as to what I wanted them to talk about.

Let us move to another conversation with children in another school conducted under different conditions. Although the children are aware why I am present and what I am interested in, we are having a more fluid conversation.

Rose Lane School

Rose Lane was not an easy school to get into. I walked around it a couple of times on my first visit before I was shouted at by a local resident hanging out of a window. She told me where the front door was. It turned out that it was locked against potentially threatening intruders. The last time I was in a primary school with locked doors was when I was evaluating bilingual education in Boston where there were racial attacks against Puerto Rican children.

We are alone. The children are talking about their view of school and they are taunting one of the four for fighting in the playground. I say something about my own memory of school.

C   *But school wasn't better then was it?*

SK *Why not, why not?*

C   *In them days schools used to be like old -*

SK *Old?*

C   *You could have like spinning-tops to play outside, we can't. We can only play hopscotch. You used to have...um... like a rope and top and you had to -*

C   *Yeh or like hula-hoop.*

I recall being taken aback. Surprised that spinning-tops were remembered - the hula-hoops are still used - that spinning-tops are thought of nostalgically! But there are confusions in this conversation. "*School wasn't better then...?*" What did they mean when they said that my school was "*old*"?

C   *I mean like, like this time now we've got computers and things like that.*

C   *We have holidays and all that but in them days you didn't used to have that...you never hardly had, like, videos like we had.*

C   *Or quite a lot of paints, like fluorescent coloured paints.*

SK *Right, what's good about school now is it's got things like computers, videos, fluorescent paint...*

C   *And holidays and all that...because I like the holidays best of all. I don't like the school.*

I am surprised again - I generally assume that primary school children enjoy school, as I did. But the others do.

C   I like school more because you get more of education from school.

SK   What does education mean?

C   Well, when you want a big job when you're older and you get more education from going to school.

C   If you want something to do with maths, you could learn it at the junior school, learn it even better at your secondary school, and get into the job when you're older.

SK   But what if there's no jobs - I mean, there's no jobs around at the moment?

C   Yes, but we'd find one somewhere.

C   Go to the Job Centre.

C   Yeh, when I'm older I'm buying a car and hopping off to Wales or somewhere.

C   Yes, that's if you pass your test because you have to pass your test before you get a car.

C   You don't!

C   You do!

I call them to order and re-focus their attention by asking them what they think education is - another 'adult' question.

C   You learn at school and when you go to your big school, you know everything in the big school.

C   No, what you do, you learn because you learn languages.

C   You don't learn languages!

C   You know school, science and that -

C   It's like you learn - you do lots of things here but maybe not the same as - like we do science here, but their science is like testing different kinds of things and we're like doing music sounds -

SK   Music sounds?

C   Like in the big school they'd be testing things like different kinds of acid -

C *I thought in this school we'd do Home Econometry - but you don't. That's cooking and things to do with your house, but we don't do it here so -*

C *We do knitting.*

Nestling in amongst general reflections of schooling and futures there is a tiny comment about our substantive concern - music in this case - unelicited by a question. There is a sense that the study of *"music sounds"* is somehow a light-weight activity compared with the science of testing and observing real matter - only a sense, because their response is not followed up.

But here is an inversion of the previous conversation with Ann's pupils. There, the context to the conversation was the music project, and within the picture being painted was the occasional detail of the girls' real experiences or values. Here the context and the substance of the conversation is a body of observations and beliefs held by the children, and appearing within it - for the briefest of moments and as a tiny detail - a snippet relevant to our substantive concern.

We are sitting in a classroom-annexe and there is a lot of noise. The children are concerned that they will not be recorded clearly. They lead me off to a quieter space. When we resume it is to talk of their fantasies for the ideal school. It resembles the present organisation of schooling - infant, junior, secondary - but locates them all on the same campus and envelops them within a giant 'leisure centre'. Another inversion. Current thinking about schools is to design them to blur boundaries between 'school' and 'community'. A new school may invite onto its campus a public library, police station, shops, theatre, a leisure centre, performing artists.

We begin to see how the Scheme slots into the lives of children. It can do so in the most dramatic way. For Asian girls, merely taking part in the project might evoke penalties in their culture of potentially alarming proportions - and yet they remain unalarmed. Children emerge in these few cases as competent evaluators of what they see around them - of the plans and actions of adults. Just as they are co-opted by educational projects, so they encapsulate those projects within their perspectives - and with relative ease.

We have seen, too, some of the bluntness and unwieldiness of the research instrument. Interview lies at the heart of evaluation because the primary evaluative act is the reflection of the individuals who participate in a project. But institutional contexts (roles and relationships) make interviews with children a very problematic exercise. We will return to that issue after the next section.

Having heard children and teachers talking, it is appropriate, now, to turn our focus on the players. They are the major initiators in these dramas and they do, as we will see, participate in AaPS projects at all levels. That is to say, they do not just initiate - they also feel the effects of events. Their experiences are just as dramatic as those of the children.

First, however, it is worth putting the players (and the Scheme) into a context appropriate to the professional culture of music. At the time of writing this account there are many initiatives to create interactions between professional music and 'community'. Some are attempts to carry music to non-concert-goers (or potential concert-goers) with the musician as the vehicle; others are attempts to broaden the experiences of professional musicians to improve their performance training. Either way, musicians are at the 'sharp end'.

Einar Solbu, Dean of Studies at the Norwegian State Academy of Music, wrote a paper (7) in which he argues the case for a new discipline of music education - one that is free of the narrow strictures of musicology, music psychology, ethnomusicology, etc. The climate, he feels, is right, given what he sees as the gradual demise of the classical music *"tradition"* and growing concerns.

"The concern is expressed in a number of ways; through actions to convert those outside the tradition and convince them of the values of the qualities of the music of the tradition, through spoken and written arguments for alternative and different musical environments than the tradition can offer, through moves to alter the educational programs for performers and other musicians, and through arguments and projects to

place the questions concerning future music life on, as it were, the general agenda."

The Scheme, as we have already seen, can be all of these, but, in the end, such initiatives do not avoid the last one in which musical questions become placed on the *"general agenda"* - ie of life. We will see this most clearly as we listen to the players give their account.

4. The Players

"I wouldn't say it changed my life, exactly," he says as we sit in the main auditorium of the Town Hall with our knees pushed up against the cinema-type seats, *"but it does make one aware of the surroundings - particularly the fact that my life in Birmingham is very channelled. I live in a very up-market area...I think it's very good for us all to visit other areas..."*

Those *"other areas"* that Rodney visits are not just geographic. He talks of his family background and current family life as one enveloped in music. *"It's a part of both myself and my wife,"* he says, and his two children are growing up in the same tradition - a pianist and a singer. But these are privileges not extended to most of the children he comes across in Birmingham schools.

Rodney is one of the wind players and on his first AaPS project - probably his last, too, since his job and his family take up all his spare time. As we leave the Town Hall, two well-known professional actors walk onto the stage loudly to prepare for tonight's performance of A *Midsummer Night's Dream* - the concert to which the AaPS schools will come. I watched them park a Rolls Royce earlier on the pavement outside. We walk down New Street - Birmingham's main shopping street - to 'Mr Spud' for a snack, and to carry on talking. There's another (string) player there, Jerry.

Rodney is saying that one of the things that comes home to him as a result of his school visits is the impact of financial policy towards schools - the poverty of resources. *"It floods my mind - that the classroom is ever so small - and there's - what - 30-odd kids packed into this classroom."* The effect, he says, must be claustrophobic. There is no library and there are virtually no musical instruments. One HMI had visited the school and declared it to be a happy school but the worst resourced he could recall. I suddenly realise that Rodney has switched to describing the school his own children go to. *"It's the sort of thing which, frankly, shouldn't be happening in a rich country like this."*

Many of the players involved in the Scheme talk about crossing divides, and the role of the Scheme in breaking down isolation, often beginning by talking about the isolation of school children who have never come in contact with concert music or with the Town Hall. But, just as often, the conversation switches to talking about the isolation of the orchestra. Jerry talks of that. She is one of the Scheme's 'veterans' and one of its advocates. *"You become much more part of the community,"* she says, and then refines the comment - *"you become part of another community - the school community as opposed to the orchestral one."*

That varies from school to school and player to player. This AaPS project had only five visits to each school so there was not a great deal of time to become immersed in the culture - other than through periodic contacts with one or two teachers and with the children. But there are degrees of immersion. For example, Lesley, one of the players, would meet her collaborating teacher in the staffroom for a coffee or lunch (she took sandwiches). This an extract from my fieldnotes.

'Here is a staffroom - the unchanging climate of schooling, always recognisable but always individual. Staffrooms are familial. This one is cramped, seats are arranged around the four walls with one chair squeezed behind the door and in the middle there are small coffee tables which mean that you have to pick your way carefully to walk from one side to another, avoiding stretched out legs. It's lunch time. A teacher is talking about her gaff during assembly and raising a great deal of laughter, *"I was talking about a man - a builder - who was filling 'craps and gacks'!"* She tells it three times as different people arrive for lunch - there is general laughter each time. There are about 8 or 10 teachers sitting eating their lunch, some bring their own and others sit with a tray on their knees eating the school meal. Today's meal is hotpot and alongside the plate with large chunks of potato and smaller chunks of meat there are little bowls with pink iced sponge cake - possibly the oldest school dinner that ever was! Some complain that the pudding is dry. *"I asked why, you know,"* one says, *"and she told me custard makes washing up harder."* This is said incredulously. *"I know! I know!"* answers another, *"so does gravy - that's why we only get it occasionally."* This is institutional life. There's much humour but a tense kind of humour that people slip into as they move from one drama to the next.

Lesley sits on the other side of the fireplace making notes, listening, with shadows of facial expressions reacting to what's being said. One of the teachers talks about having been for a couple of job interviews at other schools, but thinks that she had been invited to interview as a token experienced teacher and that in fact the job would eventually go to one of the probationers. One of the teachers doesn't cotton on to the implications of this. *"LMS! They were already trying to save money for LMS next April!"* she explains. This provokes a long conversation with people expressing stupefaction, concern, resignation. The point is that the next April will see the introduction of a new initiative under which schools will be responsible for their own budgets and heads and governors responsible for their own recruitment and staffing policies. Since everyone is expecting that this will herald tighter budgets, people are also expecting (and this teacher's experience seems to confirm) that heads will appoint the cheapest available teachers.'

Poor resourcing, low morale, unreasonable pressures and constraints from national initiatives are prominent in this account because they dominate conversations that are overheard on the AaPS. They help to create that sense of cultural difference some players experience as they talk about *"their environment"* and *"our environment"* - as they contemplate the 'divide'. These are not conversations that are directed at players, necessarily - they are spoken in their presence.

But some conversations move out to envelop the players themselves. Those players who talk to teachers about political contexts learn that the Scheme is well received by schools and generally finds a useful 'fit' with curriculum, but is threatened by the introduction of the LMS initiative. As school heads and governors become responsible for their own budgets and face tighter cash limits, they are expected to have to make choices between maths textbooks, for example, and music workshops. There are also actors, dancers, painters, environmentalists and others queuing up to compete with maths textbooks. You have to be an optimist.

But school has many faces, and noticing them - interpreting school

- is one of the things that preoccupies players. Len, a brass player, was startled. *"The school is the kids' school - not the teachers' school! Everything about it is what the kids have done...it's all their stuff!"* He remembers going to school as a child, and feeling *"I was going into the teachers' environment."* But does his view fold back on itself? What do children feel today - that school is their teachers' environment, and, possibly, Len's, too, since he is one of the grown-ups? *("So what's it like to be a pupil?"* I asked in a previous recorded moment in this account. *"I don't know,"* was the reply, *"I ain't never been a teacher,"* implying that it is the teacher who defines relationships in schools - that the adult is the reference point.)

Len, too, speaks of the isolation of the children *("they've got illusions")* and shifts, as he speaks, to talk of the isolation he feels himself. *"It's the same with us,"* he says, *"we walk on the platform and we play - then we walk off the platform and we go home."* Though Len is a fully committed performer. He went only briefly to college before taking a year off to accept an orchestral post overseas. He couldn't go back to college, so took up freelance work. And those who stayed at college? *"Well, certain people are qualified,"* he admits, *"but they really can't play. It's an ability - you can either play or you can't."* He can.

When an orchestral player walks into a school, then, who are the children seeing - how much of the person stands before them? Len gave a presentation to the children in the school hall along with Maureen. They talked about the orchestra and life in it and tried to paint a less than glamorous picture of it - but trying, too, not to undersell its mystique. Children listened attentively until concentration was sapped and they began to fidget. Questioning was a matter of cajoling and was more subdued and perfunctory than naturally inquisitive. Indeed, the presentation itself was a subdued account, talking of the sections of the orchestra, what it was like to tour, rehearsals. Nothing, that is, of the isolation or of the more controversial issues in orchestral living. Len and Maureen had to stand 'at the front' to talk while the children sat on the floor with their teachers watching over them and their voices echoing across parquet flooring and bouncing off egg-shell painted walls.

Visitors to schools walk around in a bubble of identity not of their own choosing. They are generally visiting for esoteric professional reasons in order to do something to children. So the children watch them and select from the known professional roles to label them. (*"You a governor?"* I was asked as I took notes in one class.) We will explore this a little more, keeping in mind the question of what counts as an authentic presentation of self. In what sense do children encounter, in such interactions, performing artists who are people with 'real' stories to tell, as opposed to professionals with professional stories?

Jonathan, another of the string players and, like Jerry, a veteran of a number of projects, is very committed to the educational thrust of the Scheme. The three of us are sitting in the band room back at base. We are sipping coffee from plastic cups bought in the foyer which is shared with students from the music college in the same building. *"The whole idea of the Scheme,"* he explains, *"is to try to highlight the similarities."* In the classroom making music is essentially the same activity that the orchestra is engaged in - *"people trying to make music together on different instruments"*. Jerry points to the orchestra manager sitting in the rehearsal attended by the children ostentatiously taking the orchestra register - *"it's just the same as them - we try to relate it to their normal lives"*.

But there is another side to the coin, Jonathan says, and that, too, must be explained. It is that not just anybody can do the work of an orchestral player. It's the difference between the person who plays cricket at weekends and the professional cricket player. *"What we can do which they can't actually do on their instruments - just to show a difference in standard."* He has been playing the violin since he was six. *"When you compare yourself with them, you do have an innate musicality which has been, perhaps, trampled on all over by your contemporaries at work - but when you're in a classroom full of children, you know a lot more about music than they do, so it's very uplifting for the player."*

These are contradictory views, at least as far as children are concerned. It may not be easy for a child to reconcile a message that what an orchestra does can be done inside a classroom with another message that what the orchestra does is the product of innate ability and many years of dedicated practice. In pedagogical (teaching) terms this is a contradictory message, too, requiring skilled presentation to prevent the implied élitism of the second message from downgrading the implied democracy of the first. The first message offers access - the second tends to deny it.

We are beginning to see the emergence of immediate educational dilemmas, here. Both Jonathan and Jerry, for example, use the word *"civilising"* in talking about music and the orchestral set-up. The self-discipline required, the respect for the group enterprise - *"you have to subjugate your own ego"*. Which, then, is the 'civilising' influence? The élitism (to use my own categories) or the democracy?

To say that these are contradictory views is not to imagine that Jonathan needs to resolve them - much less that a researcher or evaluator should 'launder' them to arrive at a clearer statement. Both views are authentic for Jonathan and for Jerry. People live with hopes and obligations which conflict. Part of being a professional is managing the inevitable tension between the role and the person - all professionals, by degrees, have to 'subjugate their ego'.

So contradictions are insightful for researchers. But there is a more immediate question and this is whether the contradiction itself should be part of the 'curriculum' of these Interactions. When, say, the players stand in front of children talking to them about the orchestra, ought they to be revealing the complexities in the gifts they bring with them? Should children know these things?

Most players who participated in this enquiry were concerned to bring a chunk of the real world into schools. *"It's all part of what's going on in a big city,"* said Rodney. *"Not only was it educational musically,"* Maureen said, *"it was also a social thing,"* referring to the fact that Muslim girls were able to experience places and events normally disallowed by family restrictions. *"We become ordinary people like their mums and dads and their friends,"* said Jerry. But what is the nature of the social realities these children are being exposed to?

A critical view would say that the realities in the classroom are narrowly conceived - though necessarily so given the very brief encounters we see in this Scheme. In classes there was rarely enough contact for players to move much beyond music animation. Most of the player's job in the classroom is managing the group - a common experience for short-stay visitors to the classroom. The products of two AaPS projects observed in this enquiry were confined to simplistic and socially detached imagery - through references to nature, mythology, simple emotions, etc. And formal talks were largely lectures about instruments, the orchestra, touring and classical music.

Where there are no resources to handle controversy, and no taste for it, there is a natural tendency towards low-risk and politically neutra themes. (Fairies are safer than bullies, divorcees or religious leaders - even though the latter are closer to the childrens' experience.) We have seen a mix of views and motivations in carrying music into schools and within them lie many potentially unsafe complexities. Indeed, Jonathan hinted at one when he spoke of his innate musicality having been *"trampled on"* by contemporaries. But they do not survive the journey into classrooms.

In educational terms (in terms of a curriculum which seeks to enhance children's ability and willingness to make their own judgments, as we heard teachers talking about earlier), such complexities are potentially rich material. (We have, too, heard children talking and we have seen a capacity for handling it.) Indeed, there is an elaboration of this argument which says that there are fundamental similarities in the experiences of orchestral players and children that can be explored through the medium of music-making. There are shared issues which might include:

- autonomy in the face of authority
(eg player-composer-conductor/child-teacher-text);
- the struggle of the individual against the tyranny of the group;
- competition for ownership of knowledge (who 'owns' maths or history? who 'owns' the music score?);
- judgment and assessment (both child and player are under constant public evaluation).

The point about such a list - though drawn up here arbitrarily - is tha it represents one source for a curriculum which confronts lived social realities in something of a common language. These are things about which players and children can talk and act on a basis of common experience - and it would be the players rather than the orchestra at the centre of conversations.

We see the beginnings, here, of pedagogical issues in this kind of work. Whether or not performing artists see themselves as 'teachers' (many prefer not to) there are hopes and expectations that children will learn things. *"Children should be able to express themselves in music...there's no excuse...they should be able to describe their emotions in sound,"* is the way Jonathan talks about it. The AaPS is *"educational in the same way that art and poetry in school is".* Jerry talks about the nature of the discipline required. *"If you give six children an instrument each,"* she says comparing the classroom to her string section, *"they're not going to play together by any means...you've really got to be disciplined and concentrating to do it."* Moments later she is explaining in another of those apparent contradictions that *"you have to learn to stand up by yourselves - as opposed to being one of a section".*

So who is Jerry? Teacher - player - member of a section - individual artist - citizen? She is all these and more - of course. But which facets of her and the other players do children get to see on these brief encounters? Who *is* the player?

Maggie is one of the CBSO players who has been working with the hearing-impaired children. She is a percussionist and passionate about music - *"an incredibly enriching part of my life".* She recalls her first experience with the children as 'mind-blowing'. *"...with deaf kids there's no frame of reference...they can't say 'I can hear the low sounds' - they don't know what that means. It's desperate."* She tried writing on a card 'WHAT IS MUSIC?'. *"One little girl said 'music is beautiful' - and I thought, gosh, you're dead right there girl! She didn't know what it was - but she knew that music was beautiful."*

The learning she went through continued to intrigue her. She found that deaf people have difficulty with rhythm - *"I found that staggering - you have a heartbeat, you walk in time".* But there were positive events, too, like the time she introduced some of the children to other players.

"One little girl put her hand on the bassoon and Andrew blew a low note

and she leapt back as though she'd been stung - she looked at me with eyes like stars, and she went 'oh!' again - he went up the scale and she reacted immediately."

We are sitting back at the CBSO base in the band room. Maggie sits forward in her chair - both times we met she wore a track-suit. She likes children and is close to the kids in her neighbourhood. *"At Christmas I do a lot of baking, and get the kids to come in and help me decorate - rubbish! They come in and decorate them and take the biscuits away with them. I just have fun and the place is like a tip when we've finished...it's lovely - it's an indulgence - my hobby - get locked up for that!"*

She talks easily, quickly, and doesn't wait for questions to be asked. Simon Rattle has been broadly publicised for the support he lends and Maggie talks lavishly about the requests she put in to devote ten minutes of a rehearsal, perhaps, to working with the deaf children. There was one occasion at a concert when the children from the deaf school were sitting behind the orchestra - they couldn't see Simon Rattle when he spoke to the audience. One of the children had a birthday which Simon wanted to mark - another had invented a sign for baton...'bat' and 'on'.

"Simon looked towards the audience and did this sign 'happy birthday' and said to me 'was that right?' The audience was ears out on stalks, dead silent and fascinated. I said that I didn't know, he had his back to me. A great roar of laughter. My kids began to catch on to what was happening. Then he said to the audience 'I have another sign one of the children invented, do you think you can understand it?' So he turned with his back to us again and did 'baton'. Of course Mark, the little boy who invented it nearly went berserk. Simon turned around again (Mark was behind me) and said to me 'was that all right?' I said that I couldn't see him, so I said ask Mark. Mark got up and he did it - he said it. Now for a profoundly deaf kid to actually use speech in a hall full of people - not a dry eye in the house. Incredible."

That sort of highly-charged emotional reaction was to be seen a week or so later at the rehearsal session at the sixth-form college. People often cry. But why?

"You get over that pretty quickly. It's partly wrapped up with embarrassment and ignorance and unfamiliarity and all those

things...supersensitivity and 'poor little things - isn't it a shame'. You get beyond that stage, they've got their lives and they're doing the best they can."

What about Maggie, then? Where is she at?

"I think I'm trying to prove myself in a way. Oh, yes...it's a kind of identity. If I want to be totally naked about it - yes it is, it's an indulgence."

What do you mean by identity?

"Well it makes me feel good that I am there, swan into that school, I'm their player - it's a good feeling. It gives me an identity other than sitting at the back of the orchestra counting bars and leaping off the edge of cliffs. Simon says we're all neurotics in our section, we're either waiting to jump or we've jumped."

Earlier in the interview Maggie rehearsed a number of reasons for her heavy involvement with Little Vale School. It gives her an opportunity to break down the élitism of her work - something she emphasised commenting on a draft of this piece. She - and, through her, others - comes to learn about the nature and experience of handicap. And it brings her into contact with children.

"I think it's a lot to do with the fact that I like working with children, I miss my family - they've flown the nest. Perhaps it's a substitute family - a daughter and a son. I miss them...it's lovely, I encourage them."

Why - what's lovely about kids?

"They have such marvellous, quirky ways of looking at things - open mind if you let them - if you don't talk at them and ask stupid questions all the time...it's awful - grown-ups as a breed spend their lives pestering kids with questions - they never listen to children."

The problem, of course, is communication and this is clearly one of the sources of the frustration Maggie still feels. She has not learned signing - partly the result of her own idleness, she says, and partly because there is always a class teacher present who can translate for her. But the problems still pre-occupy her.

"I think I've thought more about what I am doing over this business with the deaf kids than at any other time in my life. I'm sure the teacher wouldn't realise this but I've agonised over this for hours and hours and hours...the midnight oil that's been burnt with as many people as I can grab and talk to, I feel as though I'm seeking something...I think the

teacher suspects that I'm seeking to make those kid's hear, I suppose I am. I know they will never hear."

I prefaced this section on 'The Players' with a reference to the writing of Einar Solbu and his suggestion that music education and training break out of their narrow disciplinary confines and generate more comprehensive theories - to place music on the *"general agenda"*. He went on from there to talk about what music education should look like, how performers should be adequately prepared. *"We train our performers,"* he argues, *"to cope with unknown music, and we try to teach principles that will help them not to feel lost facing new and different scores. But we do not train them to cope with unknown and new cultural, social, emotional or communicational situations."*

In the section that follows we will look more closely at the demands that 'coping' make.

In this section, too, we have seen data mixed in with analysis. I have tried to make sense of the information at the same time as writing it down. That is a truer reflection of the way research happens. It is too easy to think of research as a set of descreet (and discrete) acts - enter the field...form hypotheses...collect data... reflect...reformulate hypotheses...more data...analyse...write... negotiate with participants...report. In reality they all happen together. You cannot collect data without knowing why - many people (I am one) carry a mental outline of a final report from the very off - an outline which serves as a measure of changing thoughts. Fieldwork - just choosing who to talk to and how - is a process of analysis. Writing is an act of analysis - data often yields up its deepest meanings under the microscope of a redraft. And the final report is just a more refined hypothesis than the very first you went in with.

But it is time to pull back from the data and to start making sense of it. We are not looking for answers here, just ways of reflecting about what we are seeing and trying to establish some patterns for thinking about it. We will start where this last section left off - with Maggie, and with the implications, not just of what she said, but of how I 'allowed' her to say it. We will return to the issue that has threaded its way through the account - how we come to understand the world of children - and make a shaky beginning at thinking about implications for curriculum.

5. The Performing Arts and Curriculum Issues

Educational Impact

What does the portrait of Maggie add to the developing analysis in this account? What do we notice in it? It is longer than the other - thumbnail sketches - of, say, Rodney and Len. It carries more (and more kinds of) data, so it is more complex - more opaque in some ways. The thumbnail sketches were used as illustrations or spring-boards for issues, whereas the portrayal of Maggie gets inside the issues to render them more sophisticated. The deeper you look, the more you elaborate, rather than explain, the issues.

The elaboration, here, takes at least two paths. One is to begin to reveal what we mean by 'educational impact' in relation to individual players. Maggie, as she talks, moves naturally between her private life, orchestral life and her experience of the deaf school (as, in a way, did Rodney). As I noted in another performing arts evaluation (8) 'outreach' projects have 'inreaching' effects.

The 'divide' - that gap in language and experience that is talked of above - is, of course, more pronounced in the case of a player working in a deaf school. We hear, from Maggie, the experience of confronting that gap - an incomplete experience, even after some years of trying. Interactions may take place in schools between adults and children playing out 'unauthentic' roles (player-teacher-pupil) but the result, in private, is unambiguously authentic - it concerns Maggie's *"identity"*.

We will pursue 'authenticity' a step further. We see evidence in this account of people being defined by the situation they find themselves in and by the expectations of, say, children. We have seen, too, that learning activities can be limited by school, that people in temporary charge of children often choose pathways (eg musical themes) which are detached from rather than connected to lived experience. Children do not get to see the players - they see versions of the players in images distorted by the filters of school.(9)

The players and the music are 'reconstituted' by school, and reconstructed in the minds of the children. There is loss of control, here.

But there is another kind of reconstruction taking place, and it is within the individual player and of themselves. *"I feel as though I'm seeking something,"* explains Maggie, as she exposes herself to demanding situations, observes, takes in data and reflects. Looking back at Jonathan we can assume that he does not pass blithely over these experiences either - especially since he has to find a way of balancing in his mind his competing hopes and values. Most of the players who participated in this enquiry spoke of their relationship with the orchestra. Leaving the orchestra to work in schools provides new data and an opportunity to reflect - it is, itself, a kind of research exercise. The reconstruction that may result is of the relationship between the player (the person) and the orchestra. That one tends to remain private.

There will be other reconstructions taking place - most people are hoping that there will be changes happening in the children - that they will be reconstructing their worlds (one definition of 'learning') to include appreciation of music or the classical tradition. We have seen teachers - Ann, for example - learning to work in different ways. Everyone, it seems, has potential for learning from this Scheme.

But people are not always learning together. Many of the questions and issues being thrown up by the AaPS remain part of a 'hidden curriculum' - at least between players and schools. The principles of partnership, mutual reflection and working for the group which underpin the pupils' music interactions do not always govern the learning process between players and pupils. One analogy which might fit comes from the Guildhall Conservatoire evaluation report referred to a moment ago. There, one observer spoke of this kind of interaction as a *"holiday camp"*. People from different cultures come together, achieve some communication in a simple common language and then go home to reflect on what they have learned about those other cultures in private. But how much could they have learned?

The implications of this kind of analysis are that there are shortfalls in communication between players and children which may prevent the culture of either group passing properly into the consciousness of the other. That ambition requires a more open form of conversation than may be reachable in brief encounters. 'Reconstruction' is a process of analysis, not a spontaneous happening, and it needs data to work. The more superficial the information people have on each other, the more superficial will be those analyses. (10)

Portrayals and Betrayals

But I wrote, a little earlier, that there were two elaborations we might make from Maggie's portrayal. We have been looking at one - the educational impact. The other concerns the children and their position in this account.

Maggie's portrayal is longer than those of the other players - but it is qualitatively different from those of the children. There are, in fact, no portrayals of children. I spoke to them in groups (I find children talk more freely in groups). They rarely emerge as individuals - indeed, I rarely give them names.

This reveals two things. Firstly, children have a different power relationship from a researcher than that enjoyed by adults and professionals. They have less control over the data - for practical reasons. Their individual expression is impaired - for practical reasons - and they emerge as smaller in every sense than Maggie, Len and Jerry. In the end, a researcher speaks to children across a similar divide as the one the players talk about. Research, too, searches for authenticity but finds itself captured by non-authentic situations - sitting in uncomfortable detachment from children who are being asked, yet again, to pretend they are pupils and not children. There is a kind of betrayal going on.

Interviews with adults are conducted in familial terms - researchers mostly spend time with professionals and can share certain key understandings (how we carry responsibility, how our ambitions are frustrated by the ways we have to work, for example). Also many of the agreements and courtesies that make a context for these interviews are unspoken - we imply them. In such interviews the researcher may be treading unknown paths, but paths which wind their ways through a familiar world, and one of the effects of research interviews like those in this account is to reaffirm our familiarity. The interview with Maggie can be reflective and self-evaluative because there is a shared language. We can identify with Maggie. We know her as we know ourselves.

Interviews with children are different. Their humour, use of aggression, the elliptical nature of their utterances seem to speak of a different world. I spend a lot of time in these interviews feeling for some kind of commonality on which to build a conversation. But common understanding rarely happens, for me, and as a result interviews with children are less reflective and require more inference and interpretation. The problem is more like that faced by anthropologists who study 'other' cultures. It's not so easy to identify with children. In this account we know children in a way we do not know ourselves.

Researchers, too, need to have the 'culture of the child' in their consciousness - not in order to return the compliment, but to communicate it to others. But there are more practical problems which are faced by adult professionals who work with children. It would help to know *how* Muslim girls feel prohibited from singing; or to understand *how* competitive, technical tasks (eg tests) often take priority with children over cooperative, creative tasks (eg music workshops); or that music can be an opportunity for children to play out their competitions. The value to musicians of these questions might be to help think about how music works as 'conversation' with children. Is music in the classroom truly like music in the Birmingham Town Hall? Can we work *alongside* children with music - or are we confined to parallel tracks? In earlier observations we saw children acting and producing music in ways which, on the face of it, are not that easy to identify with.

Passing on the Spark

This is the second time I have referred to the argument in this account provided by Bernstein, *"If the culture of the teacher,"* he wrote, *"is to become part of the consciousness of the child, the culture of the child must first be in the consciousness of the teacher."*

This implies a view of teaching as 'transaction' - an implication which has run throughout this account. Teaching is more a matter of *"negotiation"* than of *"transmission"* I wrote earlier. The reader has to beware of my own biases, of course, and though this view can be substantiated in the data, it does not reflect all the aims people hold for the AaPS. We heard, in an earlier section, the music adviser talking about 'sparking', for example, and that notion of passing on the spark of insight or creativity can be implied in what was said by Ann, the teacher, as well as in the words of players. It is a way of thinking about learning - it is a learning theory.

'Sparking' is a difficult concept to use as a working classroom guide. Informative for an individual artist, it does not easily translate into curriculum and learning strategies. It has an element of arbitrariness in it (can you plan for it?), and it is difficult to define in terms of quality and worth (we might shudder to think of some of the consequences of a Sylvia Plath passing on a 'spark'). It might even be best left uncontaminated by curriculum. In any case, CBSO players are in school for a matter of hours; children are there for years. There may well be an impact on teacher development from such encounters, as teachers (like Ann) receive a spark, but a widespread impact on children would be unreasonable to hope for.

But having mentioned teacher development, we need to be aware that the 'spark' theory of change - albeit useful for legitimising brief encounters - has a more fundamental problem in that it clashes with teachers' experiences of teaching and of classroom life. Teachers spend years with their pupils pursuing evolutionary development. But, typically, this gets translated, by even the best teachers, it seems, into immediate goals - to get *this* lesson right; to make *this* a productive day for the pupils.(11) There is no easy accommodation for spontaneous changes in direction, here - especially where changes emphasise work with individual children and require follow-up activities. In the broader context, the National Curriculum is an attempt finally to put paid to individualised approaches to learning. Spontaneous insight, personalised knowledge, serendipity - such are not the 'flavour of the month'.

Even so, there does appear to be impact on teacher development from contact with the players. It clearly requires little exposure from teachers for them to feel confident to take on music animation responsibilities - even, as in Ann's case, to re-assess one's professionalism. An earlier evaluation report from my Centre (conducted by Lawrence Ingvarson in 1989 of the Children's Music Workshop) concluded that these animateur roles were insufficient to guarantee good in-service training for teachers. Teacher learning and development required that they have access to the philosophy behind the activity - which itself requires that the artist has some kind of an educational theory underpinning what they are doing. The reasons for this will not be explored in this account, which retains its major focus on children.(12) It is worth reiterating, however, that whatever the critical tone of this account in relation to the problems of working with children, any reasonable evaluative comment on the Scheme as a whole would be positive. Schools, in particular, praised the Scheme and its contribution to cross-curricular work.

Public Knowledge

This last point raises a final perspective in this look at curriculum issues, and it concerns the obligations or otherwise on performing artists to act as teachers. I have already suggested that artists need to develop educational theories of their arts in schools activities. What lies at the heart of such an obligation?

"Prophets may teach private wisdom; teachers must deal in public knowledge," wrote Lawrence Stenhouse (13), one of Britain's leading curriculum theorists. A teacher "does not teach what he alone knows, letting his pupils in on secrets".

Performing artists - CBSO players - have no obligations to deal in public knowledge. They are sponsored to interact with schools on the basis of what they do best. Indeed, it is often letting pupils in on artistic secrets that is the nature of their task. "Many of these kids have never seen an orchestra," is commonly said. We have seen that there are broader critical questions - both of the real experience of being in an orchestra as well as of the social construction of an orchestra (orchestral players are 'divorced' from their audiences) -

which feature in conversations outside the classrooms. These questions represent Stenhouse's *"public knowledge"*.

We have seen, too, that these questions are not easily raised by players - schools may not be seen as an appropriate forum for their airing. There is a characteristic blandness to the musical themes chosen. There is a sense of peering over the edge of an adventurous moment (something 'sexy') but wanting to keep it 'safe' (perhaps born of the modern 'don't-dare-fail' idiom). And yet, we have also seen a willingness and a capacity in pupils to handle controversial information, complex issues and even political debate. What responsibilities do performing artists carry in relation to public knowledge - whether or not they see themselves as teachers? Can musicians get away with plying nothing but their trade in schools - or are they obliged to participate more fully in the educational mission? Isn't there, after all, a pedagogy - a teaching intent - behind music?

This discussion lies at the heart of this account and reflects the opening question - 'Is something that is good musically, necessarily good educationally?' The answer that comes out of this account would probably be no. What makes the AaPS educational is in the way people interact with it and make sense of it. It becomes a public 'thing' and, through inciting young Muslim girls to think or teachers to self-reflect or musicians to think about defending their work, it deals in public knowledge. Musicians might ignore that and reserve attention exclusively for the musical end of things, but they will be in the paradoxical position of having effects they are entirely unaware of.

We are approaching the end of this account. There remains one section, however, and that deals with a special case - the AaPS project with hearing-impaired children. During the course of the fieldwork (10 days in all) I came under pressure to include Little Vale School. I resisted on the grounds that it was too special ('exotic' in research parlance) to be included in a publication already pressed for space (my contract was for 20,000 to 30,000 words).

I relented, partly under pressure, but also because what was emerging as a major theme made the prospect of a visit to the school compelling. The problems of coming to grips with children across an apparent cultural divide were likely to be highlighted by attempts to teach music to hearing-impaired children. I observed an AaPS event in which Little Vale students took part and I followed them back to their school. My observations from that day (mostly fieldnotes) follow. It can be read as a sort of coda.

6. Conclusion

Innovation and Meaning in Arts Education

I wanted to end this account with children - as I began it. As my subject I chose the CBSO's work with hearing-impaired children - much publicised and very popular in the orchestra, not least with Simon Rattle. I also wanted to close by making a final statement about the AaPS and the position of such initiatives in the current educational and arts climate. How to marry the two - not an uncommon dilemma for evaluators who play many moon-spoon strategies in their report-writing! In what follows, then, there is an element of contrivance, though the more I wrote of this end-piece, the more convinced I became of its logic. Let me close, then, with two questions.

How should artists go about the business of innovation in education?

What does music-making mean to children and adults in schools?

Not long ago, Philip Jackson, a leading observer of school innovation, wrote about the arts education movement (14) sweeping the United States sponsored by the Getty Foundation - Discipline-Based Art Education (DBAE). This would be regarded by many artists and educators in Britain as a rather fusty, even old-fashioned, approach. *"In a nutshell, the key idea is that instruction in visual art from kindergarten through high school should draw upon aesthetics, art criticism, art history and art production, which are said to constitute the four foundational disciplines of art."*

Jackson was critical of the movement, partly for its conservative definition of art in education and because it was founded on notions of a sequential curriculum (highly organised and treating curriculum like building blocks) and sought to elevate the arts by making it appear more rigorous and academically respectable. *"...one way to make art instruction appear more rigorous is by treating it as a subject driven by its own internal logic, like mathematics, say."*

But why treat art like that? *"What if understanding in the arts does not develop in a neat sequential fashion? What if we were not at all sure how it develops?"*

What also puzzled him was that the advocates of DBAE *"insist on school districts as the proper unit of reform,"* rather than school buildings or classrooms. This flies in the face of the body of experience in educational innovation, which says, that the closer to the teacher and the classroom an innovation is implemented and controlled, the more impact it is likely to have - for reasons not hard to imagine.

Well, the argument is more elaborate than that, but we can infer from that a whole approach to art education which is currently fashionable in the United States - promoted by a powerful and moneyed sponsor - and which, on the face of it, resembles things as they are emerging on this side of the Atlantic with the National Curriculum. We can also begin to see, perhaps, that the potential approach to art education we have seen represented by the AaPS is a contrast.

There is represented in the AaPS an approach to innovation in art education which works close up to the action. It treats participants (teachers, players and pupils) as decision-makers. It is driven by the personal logics brought to the interactions by those individuals and it places those individuals (rather than the art) at the centre of the enterprise. I have already suggested that there may well be a tension between this kind of initiative and other contemporary approaches to school innovation. Now we can see those tensions more clearly exposed, and they arise out of fundamental differences in the way both art and innovation are seen. Here, art is a matter of experience and the art curriculum is subject to the caprices of the abilities and preferences of people.

We have, of course, seen a Scheme that has various flaws - which is vulnerable to critique from a number of angles. We might wish to measure its quality by the six aims for arts education laid out by the Gulbenkian Report (see the Introduction) and we might find it falling somewhat short, for example, in its *"exploration of values"* or in leading to *"understanding of cultural change and differences"*. We can argue against its blandness. But these flaws are there to see. The way the Scheme is organised and run exposes it, makes it accessible to critique - even invites us to make a critique. We can interact with it, and we can use it to think about how we see arts education and innovation. Through looking at this Scheme, then, we learn not only about it and about arts education, but also, if we choose, about ourselves and our own values and preferences.

What, now, of my second closing question? *What does music-making mean to adults and children in schools?* This is where I want to close with a final look at children and their teachers - in the particular case of the AaPS working with hearing-impaired children. There is, of course, no answer to the question. Meanings are held and fashioned by each individual - even then they are elusive. But the question is an important one to think about and lies at the heart of curriculum.

I have argued throughout this account - and it is a contentious point - that between children and adults there are significant differences in cultural experience. That, at the extreme, we live in our social and educational worlds in different ways. That the difference in experience between children and adults is greater than the differences between, say, two adults. Nowhere in the AaPS is that more starkly seen than in its work with hearing-impaired children. In the observation that follows we see adults communicating with children across an enormously challenging conversational gap. Musically, that gap appears almost impossibly wide - though people remain undaunted. What is happening here?

This is a speculative piece - a spur to reflection. I make no conclusions from it, I am as puzzled with the meaning of musicians working with the hearing-impaired as may be some readers. But that puzzlement over the meaning of this event reminds me that in spite of my capacity for analysing events in the AaPS and others like it, the questions raised defy easy answers. Perhaps it is important for those who work with curriculum and for those who observe it to be puzzled, but to be aware of their puzzlement and analytic of it.

That is where these two closing questions meet. The way we organise innovations helps or hinders our capacity to speculate and to learn. The more cast-iron the assumptions and the strategies which underpin innovations, the more they will limit space for critique and reflection and the more they will resist our need to learn about meanings. The more distant the source of the innovation from the classroom, the more divorced will be questions of meaning from the intentions of the curriculum. The form and content of this innovation allow us to abstract this event and to hold it up as a question. Whose meanings matter?

Little Vale Hearing-Impaired School

The boy rejects the woman and moves on to the next. He lifts the long hair on the side of her head, examines her ears, lets it fall as though it were a flap, shakes his head and moves on again. He is 12 or 13 years old - an Asian youth. She is 29. It is her birthday today - she is his music teacher.

He moves to confront another woman. This woman stands behind a large bass drum. She is a woman in her late forties and blonde. She wears a track-suit. It is Maggie. He waves a dismissive hand and moves on. She raises an eyebrow.

Now he comes to a young girl - one of his contemporaries. He looks her up and down, bends forward arching his body across the distance between them and examines her teeth. He turns away, waving the same dismissive hand over his shoulder and moves on to the next. Perfunctory passes at two boys bring him to another girl at whom he looks, screws up his face in distaste and makes an even more emphatic gesture of rejection.

Moments later he stands in front of another girl. She is tall. She has Asian colouring, her black hair is long, pulled back from her face and tied in a tress at the back. She wears dark blue school uniform with a blue cardigan and black pants which reach down to her shoes. Where the other girls and women have put on a face expressing disappointment at his rejection, this girl shows just a flicker of satisfaction at being approved. He takes her hand, leads her to the centre of the circle and walks away.

There is silence. Two girls appear at each side of the chosen one

music room and file down a busy corridor with their instruments, trying to keep contact with each other so as not to lose their way. They are all in school uniform and stand out amongst the college students who make a constant flow up and down the staircase, dressed as they would wish and many in modern styles.

Down on the second floor the group files into the main assembly hall - a very large space, with plate glass windows on each side, allowing the brilliant light of a low winter sun to stream across the room. There are about 150 children and adults in the hall - children of all ages. There are five schools represented here including the college itself.

As the morning proceeds the children and their teachers from each school make a musical presentation. The Scheme this term is based on Stravinsky's *Rite of Spring* and was initiated by Richard McNicol (a freelance professional music animateur and an ex-member of the Royal Philharmonic Orchestra) with a one-day teachers' workshop. Since then, teachers have worked with CBSO players for three visits, preparing a musical presentation from each of the schools which will be performed in a small hall in the centre of the city. The night before, everyone will go to the concert at the Town Hall to hear the CBSO play the piece. This is the schools' rehearsal.

There are school advisers here and an audience of students from the college. At one end sits Janet's group, quiet in the mêlée waiting for their turn. When it comes they are sandwiched between a secondary school and a primary school. Their performance is met with 'yowls', clapping and whistling.

At the end of the session the hall empties slowly. All have passed this testing experience including Janet's group. One adult observer is emphatic about them. *"They were nervous!"* she says, *"They weren't sure whether their piece was any good! It was amazing! We sat there with tears streaming down our faces! They were not sure that it was any good and there we were crying our hearts out! Fantastic!"*

Why do people cry in these situations?

Bibliography

Clem Adelman (1987) 'The Arts and Young Children' chapter in *The Arts in Education: Some Research Studies* Les Tickle (ed.), Croom Helm

Clem Adelman (1989) *Play as a Quest for Vocation,* mimeo, Faculty of Education, University of Reading

Michael Armstrong (1981) *Closely Observed Children,* Writers and Readers

Douglas Barnes & Frank Todd (1977) *Communication and Learning in Small Groups,* Routledge & Kegan Paul

Gill Barrett (1986) *Learning in the School Process,* PhD Thesis, University of East Anglia, Norwich NR 7TJ

Basil Bernstein (1970) 'A Critique of the Concept of Compensatory Education', chapter in *Education for Democracy,* Rubinstein, D & Stoneman, C (eds.), Penguin Books

Martyn Denscombe (1980) 'Pupil Strategies in the Open Classroom', chapter in *Pupil Strategies: explorations in the sociology of the school,* P Woods (ed.), Croom Helm

Henry A Giroux (1989) *Schooling for Democracy: Critical Pedagogy in the Modern Age,* Routledge (London)

Lawrence Ingvarson (1989) *An Interim Evaluation of the Children's Music Workshop at Thornhill Primary School,* CARE mimeo, University of East Anglia, Norwich NR4 7TJ

Philip Jackson (1968) *Life in Classrooms,* Holt, Rhinehart & Winston Inc (NY)

Philip Jackson (1987) 'Mainstreaming Art: an Essay on Discipline-Based Art Education', article in *Educational Researcher,* Vol 16 No 6 Aug-Sept

Saville Kushner (1988) *A Musical Education: Innovation in the Conservatoire,* final report of the Guildhall (MPCS) evaluation, CARE mimeo, University of East Anglia, Norwich NR4 7TJ

Jack Sanger (1988) 'The Magic Box of Delights' chapter in *Breaking into the Curriculum*, John Schostak (ed.), Methuen (London)

Ann Saunders (1987) *A Process in Mind*, PhD Thesis, University of East Anglia, Norwich NR4 7TJ

Ronald Silvers (1975) 'Discovering Children's Culture', mimeo, Ontario Institute for Studies in Education, Canada

Ronald Silvers (1986) 'From the Light of Children's Art' article in *Phenomenology and Pedagogy*, Vol 4 No 2

Einar Solbu (1987) *Empty Spaces on Stage: Research and Training of Performers in a Musical Environment*, mimeo, Norwegian State Academy of Music, Oslo

Robert Stake (1975) *Evaluating the Arts in Education: a Responsive Approach*, Charles E Merrill Publishing Company (Ohio)

Lawrence Stenhouse (1975) *An Introduction to Curriculum Research and Development*, Heinemann (For the OU)

Keith Swanwick (1988) *Music, Mind and Education*, Routledge (London, NY)

Veronica Treacher (ed.) (1988) *Assessment and Evaluation in the Arts*, Collaborative Action research report, Berkshire LEA, Shire Hall, Shinfield Park, Reading

Notes

I Robert Stake, *Evaluating the Arts in Education: a Responsive Approach* (1975), Charles E Merrill Publishing Company, Ohio, USA.

2 *The Arts in Schools: principles, practice and provision* (1982), Calouste Gulbenkian Foundation, London, UK.

3 The matter does not end there, of course, and there is much empirical research on children's thinking and learning - not least in relation to arts education. Examples include Silvers (1975, 1986) who takes an ethnographic and psychological view (*"how we may reachieve a social bond between children and adults by surpassing the boundaries of an adult's interpretive universe..."*); Swanwick (1988) who offers a theoretical developmental model of learning in music education; PhD theses by Gill Barrett (1986) and Ann Saunders (1987) on children's thinking and creativity; Veronica Treacher (1988) who edited teachers' own accounts of coming to grips with these problems in the Berkshire 'Arts in Schools Project'; and Michael Armstrong (1981) who has published much of his own observations of children's self-expression through art in the classroom.

4 Indeed, there is a research literature on precisely this scenario. Denscombe (1980) for example, argues that *"to a greater or lesser extent, the social order of the classroom is a negotiated phenomenon with pupils and teachers adopting strategies which promote their particular interests"*. Sanger (1988) looks at children in self-directed classroom activities and at how they shift roles, periodically becoming their own teachers under rules and rituals which are - given their reluctance to elaborate in conversation - elusive to adult observers. Sanger's is one of the more insightful and sustained observations of this kind and he works hard on revealing the order underlying apparently *"Luddite"* interactions.

5 *"This 'gap' or 'silence'...between adults' culture and children's culture,"* says Adelman (1987) *"recurs in conversations about children's own*

constructions. The adult searches for the children's referents, often unsuccessfully."

6 Clem Adelman (1989) looks at the nature of and differences between 'work' and 'play' in curriculum and in relation to learning. "Play entails self-discipline," he writes, "...a true and relevant way of learning."

7 Entitled Empty Spaces on Stage: Research and Training of Performers in a Musical Environment. It was written during a sabbatical period at the Eastman School of Music, New York.

8 Kushner (1988) The final report of a three-year evaluation of an innovatory course in a conservatoire. Students left the conservatoire to conduct music workshops in community institutions and brought back with them questions for themselves and questions for their college curriculum.

9 Lawrence Stenhouse (1975), for example, talked of the "professional persona, often the result of tension between the stereotyped role of the teacher and the real person who fills it..." Nonetheless, Stenhouse was the leading advocate of curriculum development based on teacher development - out of which sprang the 'teacher-as-researcher' movement. The question raised, of course, is whether teacher-development is feasible as anything other than personal development - which is why Ann's testimony, here, is so interesting.

10 There is a more fundamental critique from radical curriculum theorists. Giroux (1989), for example, argues "by analysing culture uncritically either as an object of veneration or as a set of practices that embody the traditions and values of diverse groups, this...depoliticises culture". He argues for a "critical pedagogy" based upon the emancipatory approach of Paulo Freire - to "understand culture as shared and lived principles of life...within inequitable relations". Stenhouse (1975), too, argues that we need a more "sinuous conception of culture to do justice to the way in which it is shared and distributed".

11 Philip Jackson (1968) wrote one of the classic observational studies of classrooms and teaching during which he interviewed 50 "outstanding" teachers. "Although teaching might be thought of as being

chiefly concerned with...producing invisible changes within the student - this select group of teachers did not rely very much on pious hopes of reaping an 'unseen harvest'," he said. But, furthermore, teachers are too familiar with classrooms to move beyond monitoring this pupil at this time. "This degree of specificity greatly inhibits the easy translation of theory into practice."

12 There is available from CARE, University of East Anglia, the evaluation report of a similar music project at a primary school in Islington which focusses specifically on the impact of such schemes on the professional development of teachers (Ingvarson, 1989). Ingvarson, being an experienced teacher-educator is sceptical about the value of expert-led, 'flying-visit' approaches to in-service training, but records some similar results in that school. "The key professional development issue," he says, however, "is whether the teachers have gained a personally meaningful idea of the musicians' approach to music education, or only a grasp of how to repeat more or less what the musicians did."

13 Stenhouse (1975) He was introducing an argument that schools carried obligations to introduce pupils to public traditions - to 'a selection of society's intellectual, emotional and technical capital".

14 Philip Jackson (1987) 'Mainstreaming Art: an essay on Discipline-Based Art Education' in Educational Researcher Vol 16 No 6 Aug-Sept.